# ORGANIZING ANARCHY

# Studies in Critical Social Sciences Book Series

Haymarket Books is proud to be working with Brill Academic Publishers (www.brill.nl) to republish the *Studies in Critical Social Sciences* book series in paperback editions. This peer-reviewed book series offers insights into our current reality by exploring the content and consequences of power relationships under capitalism, and by considering the spaces of opposition and resistance to these changes that have been defining our new age. Our full catalog of *SCSS* volumes can be viewed at https://www.haymarketbooks .org/series_collections/4-studies-in-critical-social-sciences.

# ORGANIZING ANARCHY

## Anarchism in Action

### JEFF SHANTZ

Haymarket Books
Chicago, IL

First published in 2019 by Brill Academic Publishers, The Netherlands
© 2019 Koninklijke Brill NV, Leiden, The Netherlands

Published in paperback in 2021 by
Haymarket Books
P.O. Box 180165
Chicago, IL 60618
773-583-7884
www.haymarketbooks.org

ISBN: 978-1-64259-362-4

Distributed to the trade in the US through Consortium Book Sales and
Distribution (www.cbsd.com) and internationally through Ingram Publisher
Services International (www.ingramcontent.com).

This book was published with the generous support of Lannan Foundation and
Wallace Action Fund.

Special discounts are available for bulk purchases by organizations and
institutions. Please call 773-583-7884 or email info@haymarketbooks.org for more
information.

Cover design by Jamie Kerry and Ragina Johnson.

Printed in the United States.

10 9 8 7 6 5 4 3 2 1

Library of Congress Cataloging-in-Publication data is available.

*Dedicated to*
*Molly Shantz, Saoirse Shantz, and Eva Ureta*

# Contents

# Acknowledgements

It should first be acknowledged that I live, work, and organize, on the unceded (that is, stolen) territories of the Coast Salish Peoples, where most of the writing of the book was done.

I would like to recognize and thank all of the people working to organize anarchism and striving to build better worlds beyond the Earth destroying capitalist system of exploitation and control—and its statist facilitators. And who are creating real world supports to make alternatives possible. This includes the people organizing to defend our communities from assault by rising forces of authoritarianism and neofascism. I would like to thank especially those I have worked with directly in numerous projects over decades, including but not limited to projects that are discussed in this book.

In particular I would like to thank Eva Ureta for ongoing love and support. This book benefitted greatly from conversations with Eva over many days and nights of discussion, including many late nights at the all-night café Breka on Davie and Granville in Vancouver. It would not have been the same without her inspiration and enthusiasm and without the perspective developed over many conversations (and laughs and smiles) with Eva throughout. Her joyful energy, support, and encouragement have lifted me.

I must thank Molly and Saoirse Shantz for their support and for being such wonderful folks to share a household—and a world—with. They have generously allowed me much time to do the work that I do.

Thank you as well to David Fasenfest, the Critical Social Sciences series editor, for supporting active, engaged, critical scholarship and research with such dedication.

This is an exciting period of anarchist organizing, and anti-capitalist organizing more broadly. There are so many grounded and inspiring projects of mutual aid and solidarity building bases for durable positive social transformation, defending communities today and building new relations for tomorrow. I hope the discussions here do right by them while also offering some additional inspiration and insight.

# Introduction

This is a book about organizing in a supposedly unlikely source—anarchist movements. It is about organizing anarchy, a notion that would seem a contradiction to many. Anarchism is caricatured as the ultimate form of disorganization or non-organization. In writing this I set out partly to provide something of a corrective to much activist, popular, and academic thinking about anarchism. At the same time I hoped to inspire activists, anarchist and non-anarchist, to see anarchism anew. These are still aims and intentions underlying this work. But now there is a new urgency, a new sense of necessity about its appearance.

A not so funny thing happened on the way to publishing this book. The election of Donald J. Trump as President of the United States of America, the culmination of a startling period starting with the party primaries through the presidential race, changed the context of political analysis and debate. In dramatic ways. In only the first week of the Trump administration a member of one of the organizing examples discussed in this book, the Industrial Workers of the World, was shot by a Right-wing supporter of white nationalist Milo Yiannopoulos at a protest against the Right provocateur's performance at the University of Washington in Seattle.

The Trump election served as a bucket of ice water in the face of progressive activists of various stripes causing a renewal of radical discussion and argument over the need to organize serious resistance to the Right-wing forces—white supremacy, corporatism, proto-fascism, violent nationalism—unleashed and energized by the Trump campaign and election. These forces of violent reaction seemed poised to build and expand beyond the lifetime of any Trump presidency.

On the one hand the Trumpist movements and forces have impelled a rethinking of the limits of traditional electoral politics and recognition of the failings of progressive engagement with the formal parties and party systems whether Democratic, Green, Libertarian, or other.

On the other hand radical activists have been forced, like they have not had to in decades, to address issues of sustainable resistance and durable organization. Suddenly protests and demonstrations do not seem like nearly enough for more and more people. Indeed, they seem as much as ever to be futile gestures in the face of a rising, active, aggressive—and organized and resourced—far Right wing, what some would call proto-fascist mobilization.

Many have turned to extra-parliamentary politics for the first time seeking alternatives to a system of passive democracy that leaves them voiceless even during the election period in which they might in some way be canvassed. They seek alternative forms of political organization and practice and new outlets for raising their voices and concerns.

Others have been newly radicalized and seek to move politics in a manner that seems suited to the times. They have grown frustrated with politics that, even where oppositional, fail to get to the roots of social problems or which pose no real, sustained challenge to the status quo, or the new post-Trumpist abnormal.

Even seasoned activists have come to question previously comfortable practices that once inspired hope, or raised a promise of change, but which now seem overwhelmed or hopeless, based still on making appeals to power or seeking to register dissent rather than posing and preparing alternatives.

Among the most radical or farthest going expressions of alternative politics have been provided by anarchist movements. Yet the popular and stereotypical biases against anarchism have left anarchist alternatives obscured or overlooked or unrecognized. These stereotypes—of anarchism as chaos and disorder, of anarchism as mere violence or confrontation—are far from the reality of actual anarchist movements and projects.

This book gets past the stereotypical and caricatured, the dismissive and contemptuous representations of anarchism. It also focuses on aspects of anarchism that have been largely overlooked by popular media and academic studies alike. The experiments in organizing presented here even go beyond the more dramatic actions, insurrectionism, rebellion, subcultural expressions, focused on by many activists themselves.

The organizational practices and sites of struggle presented here show the incredible range of anarchist practice and vision. From community centers and alternative spaces, to workplace resistance, to cyber disobedience online. They also show the great range of issues and concerns that motivate anarchism and anarchists. From work to education to psychological health and wellbeing to communications, anarchists have developed practical alternatives.

This organized anarchism, far from being a contradiction, shows a serious and mature movement thinking and acting to meet peoples' real world needs in the here and now of everyday life—as well as pointing to new futures and ways of relating and acting. And they do so while providing real material, emotional, physical, psychological resources and infrastructures for resistance. Far from the inchoate chaos and disorder they are accused of being by critics, mass media and academics alike, anarchists organize with a purpose and with a point. They work hard, and play hard, in doing so.

This book, and the examples discussed within it, provide a resource for all of those seeking to understand and assess new forms of political practice and approaches to organizing as well as those seeking alternatives to the present order of things.

# CHAPTER 1

# Another Kind of Order: Anarchism against the State

*ANARCHY*

> *Ever reviled, accursed, ne'er understood,*
> *Though art the grisly terror of our age.*
> *"Wreck of all order," cry the multitude,*
> *"Art thou, and war and murder's endless rage."*
> *O, let them cry. To them that ne'er have striven.*
> *The truth that lies behind a word to find,*
> *To them the word's right meaning was not given.*
> *They shall continue blind among the blind.*
> *But thou, O word, so clear, so strong, so pure,*
> *Thou sayest all which I for goal have taken.*
> *I give thee to the future! Thine secure*
> *When each at least unto himself shall waken.*
> *Comes it in sunshine? In the tempest's thrill?*
> *I cannot tell—but it the earth shall see!*
> *I am an Anarchist! Wherefore I will*
> *Not rule, and also ruled I will not be!*

  JOHN HENRY MACKAY

∵

Leonard Krimerman and Lewis Perry tell a story, perhaps apocryphal, of the months that passed in the early days of the young United States during which arguments among delegates stalled the Pennsylvania constitutional convention designated to establish a new government. During this period Benjamin Franklin is said to have offered assembled delegates the following warning:

> Gentlemen, you see that in the anarchy in which live society manages much as before. Take care, if our disputes last too long, that the people do not come to think that they can very easily do without us.
>
>   quoted in KRIMERMAN and LEWIS 1996, xv

While the remark was made in jest by a man who would have dreaded the loss of government, it points out the key challenge raised consistently by anarchists and highlights a great, persistent fear of political rulers. That is that given the opportunity, regular people can, and likely will, organize their lives efficiently and sufficiently to meet their own needs and interests, without disruption or dislocation, crisis or calamity. At the same time, it is clear that in the current period of global neoliberal capitalism this challenge is not at the moment one that presses up against the real power, control, and domination exercised by political—and economic—elites and rulers.

With the advent of the welfare state in liberal democracies during the middle of the twentieth century the state has assumed greater social functions and come to intervene in growing areas of social interaction, including morality and culture. There has been a notable expansion of government power and growth of the administrative bureaucracies. Examples include public power, crop prices, housing, and education. This is a development of capitalist modernity remarked upon by sociologists from Weber through Mills to the present period.

The reach of government institutions has become expansive—even global in the case of agencies such as the North Atlantic Treaty Organization (NATO), the Asia Pacific Economic Cooperation (APEC), the United Nations (UN), or the World Trade Organization (WTO). In domestic realms, government has claimed responsibility for the social regulation of a wide range of activities, from consumption practices to sexual activities, medicine to mortgages, gambling and online communication.

In the twenty-first century, the reach of governments has expanded into a range of spheres of global activity. This is well illustrated in the capacity of the US government to roam halfway around the world, slip into a country like Pakistan and assassinate a political opponent. This reach has even extended beyond the bounds of planet earth, extending into the atmosphere through satellite surveillance and space stations, and into deeper space through explorer drones and telescopes.

Many would view the potential collapse of these highly structured systems to be fantastic, the realm of science fiction or futuristic fiction. Others would view such a circumstance as entirely frightful—merely contemplating it would be filled with anxiety and tension—intertwined as their own lives have become with state institutions and practices.

Still, the specter of anarchy continues to pose the very nightmare scenario that so haunts political rulers, and which served as the motivation for Ben Franklin's nervous joke. That the promise of anarchy still serves to frighten political rulers is currently reflected in the great mass of resources (police, laws, courts, and prisons) deployed by governments to suppress anarchist movements and groups within the recent alternative globalization and, even more recent, Occupy movements of the early twenty-first century. Entering the last decades of the twentieth century, modern governments had seemingly stamped out or dampened many of the impulses that gave rise to anarchist movements. Examples of the criminalization of anarchy abound from so-called criminal anarchy laws in the 1910s, the Red Scare of 1919, and the deportations of anarchists up through the attacks on black bloc anarchists by police today.

## 1    The Anarchist Seed Beneath the Statist Snow

Yet, despite all of this, anarchy has survived, as Colin Ward has suggested, like a "seed beneath the snow." Hibernating in the cold winter of the state, anarchy breaks through and rises to the surface, blooming to show alternative ways of organizing life.

During the 1960s and 1970s the peace, anti-war, civil rights, anti-nukes, and environmental movements shared strong affinities with anarchism. Often, they explicitly drew upon and engaged with anarchist ideas, politics, and histories. In many cases they adopted practices, such as affinity group structures, participatory democracy, and direct action, which had characterized anarchist organizing historically. Anarchism maintained an active presence, punching above its weight in anti-capitalist and anti-imperialist movements, through the 1980s. Much of the anarchist revival in the 1980s was driven on a subcultural level through the scenes of punk music, art, and activism. Urban squatting and anti-fascist struggles played important parts. Since the 1990s anarchism has enjoyed a vital revival initially through alternative globalization movements but expanding well beyond that in a range of expressions, interests, and directions.

Criticism of the authoritarianism, brutality, and suppression of freedom exhibited in so-called socialist states has long encouraged progressive, or Left, critics to turn to anarchism as an alternative revolutionary tradition rooted in liberty and equality, but consistently opposed to capitalist exploitation and domination. Indeed, anarchists were some of the first critics of the Soviet regime in Russia—and among its first victims.

Many people, even within contemporary liberal democracies, have become suspicious of the state, viewing it as wasteful and incompetent at best and repressive and brutal at worst. This suspicion of the state has taken the form—on the Right—of militia groups and the Tea Party. Those who seek to limit the state's perceived (usually financial) excesses often wind up calling for a nostalgic return to an imagined "purer" monarchist state form. This is the idea of the state as solely a night watchman involved only in matters of domestic security and military defense of sovereign borders. The Right critics, often under the banner of libertarianism in North American contexts, are typically not motivated by sentiments of equality and commonality but rather by pursuit of their own economic interests. They can be exclusionary and xenophobic in their visions and practices.

Some others who have developed approaches that might be termed anti-statist have turned instead to community building, alternative institutions, and voluntary associations to seek alternatives to the state. These approaches are most closely associated with contemporary anarchism.

Anarchism becomes more relevant again in the era of neoliberal capitalism. Once again, the state in capitalist societies is positioned—not as a provider of social services that meets important needs of the working classes and poor—but as a mechanism for the advantage of capital. The neoliberal state is more readily recognizable as a mechanism of oppression of the many for the few—and institution of class rule. When governments in Western liberal democracies find billions of dollars in times of economic crisis to bail out banks and companies that are deemed "too big to fail" at the same time as they impose social service cuts and austerity budgets on working people and the poor, people's appraisal of the state becomes more critical. The state is recognized as an instrument of injustice and inequality for many. In the language of the Occupy movement the state is positioned as a protector of the 1% against the interests and needs of the 99%. Though anarchists tend to think in terms of class rather than percents, the analyses overlap in numerous ways.

Given the sense that there are few, if any, alternatives to capitalism, and the broad misunderstanding about what anarchism actually means, contemporary anarchists seek to change public attitudes. They seek to change the social climate in which ideas might be received and discussed. As Paul Goodman suggests:

> Police courts and administrative officers, however, and even jury courts and high courts, are hardly the right forum for important and subtle moral debates. (1966, 54)

Goodman makes the distinction between society, a collection of persons, and the community of human beings (1966, 55). On the need for preparedness in countering the expansion of state grasp, the individualist anarchist Benjamin Tucker argues:

It has ever been the tendency of power to add to itself, to enlarge its sphere, to encroach beyond the limits set for it; and where the habit of resisting such encroachment is not fostered, and the individual is not taught to be jealous of his rights, individuality gradually disappears and the government or State becomes the all-in-all. (1966, 66)

For anarchists, the new society can and must be made now. It is not something to be left to the future. The future society must be made in the present. The end of the state allows for the flourishing of alternatives. These alternatives are based on distinct types or social arrangements. In the words of Mackay:

When this individual awakes to life, the knell of the State has sounded: society takes the place of government; voluntary associations for definite purposes, the place of the State; free contract, the place of statute law. (1966, 21)

Meeting this promise means people must have experiences with other ways of doing things beyond the archic hierarchical, violent structures of states and capital. Thus, despite the clichéd caricatures of anarchism as disorder or chaos, anarchists are active in a range of social projects by which they seek to build resources to oppose current structures and institutions they view as oppressive and repressive, but also to build experiences in alternative ways of doing things. They are, in this, organizing anarchy, today, in the here and now of everyday life.

## 2      Anarchy Is Order

Opposition always places enormous obstacles in the path of new ideas. Great tools of repression have been invented to impede the progress of movements for justice. As the anarchist Vaillant declared at his trial more than a century ago: "Too long have they answered our voices by imprisonment, the rope, rifle volleys." At the same time less obtrusive and aggressive methods have been deployed to discredit and dismiss social visions that challenge the status quo.
   As Emma Goldman suggests:

Anarchism could not hope to escape the fate of all other ideas of innovation. Indeed, as the most revolutionary and uncompromising innovator, Anarchism must needs meet with the combined ignorance and venom of the world it aims to reconstruct. (1969, 48)

Anarchism, as the most thoroughgoing opposition to authority has been sub-jected to some of the most thoroughgoing attempts by constituted authorities, in states and business, to remove it from the realm of social discourse.

Before any movement or organization emerged to promote anarchism, rulers—those constituted authorities that anarchism rejects—had rather suc-cessfully distorted the word into meaning simply chaos and disorder. This is not particularly surprising given that constituted authorities have the most to lose from a rise in anarchy in its initial sense. Such distortions are not without precedent in political history, of course. As the anarchist Errico Malatesta has noted:

> In those epochs and countries where people have considered govern-ment by one man (monarchy) necessary, the word *republic* (that is, gov-ernment of many) has been used precisely like *Anarchy*, to imply disor-der and confusion. (1891, 4)

Anarchism has been reduced to what Krimerman and Perry describe as "a gal-lery of outlandish stereotypes" (1966, xvi). The litany of caricatures and exam-ples of dismissive comments are virtually without end. A primary charge lev-eled against anarchism by those seeking to dismiss it, is that it is impractical. For critics, anarchism is a perhaps beautiful, perhaps hopeful dream, but one that is ultimately doomed to failure. The most common caricature of anar-chism is that it stands for chaos, disorder, and, above all, disorganization.

Anarchy is routinely depicted and dismissed as wanton violence and pre-sented as a knee jerk destructive impulse. It is conflated with nihilism and por-trayed as a philosophy for those who simply want to smash. A common joke goes as such: "How many anarchists does it take to change a lightbulb? None, the lightbulb must be smashed!" To be sure this image is reinforced in popular expressions that anarchists themselves have taken up. Many young people were brought to anarchism through punk music and lyrics such as those of the Sex Pistols in "Anarchy in the UK": "Don't know what I want/But I know how to get it." Or "I want to destroy."

Anarchists are most often portrayed as individual rebels. They have often been presented as loners and social outcasts who seek to destroy bourgeois society one bomb at a time. Such depictions date from the period of the late nineteenth and early twentieth centuries when some people did engage in acts of assassination against political and economic elites behind the banner of an-archy. Such acts were carried out by very few individuals and they were largely condemned by anarchist movements internationally.

In the words of Bertrand Russell:

> In the popular mind...an Anarchist is a person who throws bombs and commits other outrages, either because he is more or less insane, or because he uses the pretense of extreme political opinions as a cloak for criminal proclivities.
>
>                 quoted in NOVAK 2010, 20

Anarchism is presented as a danger, as something to be feared. It is made to represent a monstrous figure. It serves as a social boogeyman to scare the public.

The orthodox Marxist George Plekhanov refers to anarchism anarchist organizing as grotesque fancifulness. For Plekhanov, anarchist tactics offer little more than pageants of futility, decadence, and obstruction (1966, 495). In his view, anarchists, by avoiding political parliamentary action, have no recourse except to engage in limited acts of violence. Plekhanov is led to the caricature of anarchists as desperate bomb throwers. For Plekhanov, the anarchist:

> He wants the revolution, a "full, complete, immediate, and immediately economic" revolution. To attain this end he arms himself with a saucepan full of explosive materials, and throws it amongst the public in a theatre or a café. He declares this is the "revolution." For our own part it seems to us nothing but "immediate" madness. (1966, 498)

Of course, many of the so-called conspiracies of which anarchists have been accused have turned out to be manufactured. In the present-day context of alternative globalization protests as in the nineteenth century, acts violence attributed to anarchists have actually been perpetrated by members of police departments. As presiding Judge Gary said of the Haymarket martyrs: "Not because you have caused the Haymarket bomb, but because you are anarchists, you are on trial" (Diehl and Donnelly 2003, 58).

The violence carried out by anarchists historically is miniscule when compared with the violence inflicted by economic and political elites. Emma Goldman points out:

> Compared with the wholesale violence of capital and government, political acts of violence are but a drop in the ocean. That so few resist is the strongest proof how terrible must be the conflict between their souls and unbearable social iniquities. (1969, 107)

Even more positive portrayals also fixate on the individual anarchist figure rather than anarchist organizations or collectivities. This time the anarchist is presented as a living example of the proper life. Typically this depiction shows the anarchist as a humble esthete. The anarchist is, thus, one who has withdrawn from social organization and society more broadly to pursue a quiet life of self-reflection and self-fulfillment. Examples include the peasant turn of Leo Tolstoy and the chosen poverty of Catholic Workers Dorothy Day and Ammon Hennacy. These are portrayals of the anarchist not as terrorist but as its diametrical opposite—the anarchist as saint. The noble anarchist.

Even those who have sincerely engaged with anarchist ideas have fallen into mistaken representations and arguments over false constructions of anarchy. Bertrand Russell identifies anarchists as hasty reasoners in their calls for abolition of the law and government (as institutions of the state). Russell misunderstands anarchy as a situation in which every individual is free to follow their every impulse. For Russell, the state is necessary for certain central purposes. Yet, the purposes he lists include war, tariffs, and restrictions on liquor sales. These are hardly aspects of social life that anarchists would view as essential or central. For Russell, consumption must be regulated by the state "and some degree of legal restriction seems imperative for the national health" (1966, 494). He is concerned about supposedly disastrous increases in drunkenness in the absence of laws that restrict liquor traffic and the absence of liquor taxes.

Yet anarchists have been little interested in nations or their preservation—much less their health. Russell suggests that the state ensures "a just system of distribution" despite the role of the state in maintain unequal property relations, protecting the exploitation of workers by capital, and practices of usury by lending agencies (1966, 494). Anarchists point out that the state maintains the unjust system of wealth distribution under state capitalist economies.

At least Russell got some things right about anarchism. On crime and justice, and the anarchist critique, Russell notes:

> At present a very large part of the criminal law is concerned in safeguarding the rights of property, that is to say—as things are now—the unjust privileges of the rich. Those whose principles lead them into conflict with government, like Anarchists, bring a most formidable indictment against the law and the authorities for the unjust manner in which they support the *status quo*. Many of the actions by which men have become rich are far more harmful to the community than the obscure crimes of poor men, yet they go unpunished because they do not interfere with the existing order. (1966, 494)

Another prominent critic of anarchism was the Fabian socialist George Bernard Shaw. Unlike most other critics of anarchism, Shaw recognized that there is great diversity in anarchist positions rather than their being an anarchist position in the singular. Even more, Shaw does not oppose anarchist aims and principles. In his view, anarchists share with Fabian socialists broad interests in justice and cooperation. His criticism is specifically focused on the methods and practical measures that anarchists advocate. His is a criticism of anarchist organizing. Shaw, like other critics, envisions anarchism as a negative program.

Shaw divides anarchism into what he sees as its two main currents— individualist and communist—and offers specific arguments against each. These two currents in anarchism, and debates and disagreements over organizing practices will be discussed in the next chapter. Shaw's discussion of individualist anarchism is limited to notions of the price of labor in Tucker and Proudhon and is of less concern to us here.

Shaw's criticism of communist anarchism is that it relies too much on public opinion to achieve desired outcomes—having no other means of compulsion. Yet this criticism rests on his lack of awareness of real-world anarchist practices and projects, reflected in his complete lack of mention of constructive forms of organized anarchy. In his view:

> I submit, then, to our Communist Anarchist friends that Communism requires either external compulsion to labor, or else a social morality which the evils of existing society shew that we have failed as yet to attain. I do not deny the possibility of the final attainment of that or any other degree of public conscience; but I contend that the path to it lies through a transition system which, instead of offering fresh opportunities to men of getting their living idly, will destroy those opportunities altogether, and wean us from the habit of regarding such an anomaly as possible, much less honorable. (1966, 509)

Yet these transition systems are largely what anarchist communists work to provide in the form of infrastructures of resistance or what the anarchist sociologist Howard Ehrlich calls anarchist transfer cultures (see Shantz 2010).

In response to Shaw, and his belief in that the state might be reformed through Fabianism, the anarchist Emma Goldman wryly remarked that Shaw "hopes for the miraculous from the State" (1969, 58). Indeed, for anarchists, it is the liberals and social democrats who imagine the state as something other than a monstrous upholder of inequality and violent defender of injustice who are truly utopia dreamers. Turning the tables somewhat they ask: "Where are the examples of states that have acted otherwise; where the states that are not founded on the monopoly on violence?"

## 3      Constructive Anarchy

Anarchists from at least Kropotkin in the 1890s have defined anarchism not only as a movement but as a social theory (Krimerman and Perry 1966, 3). For the most part, anarchism has grown to represent a set of theories rather than a single theory. As Krimerman and Perry have suggested, defining anarchism

> ...involves identifying principles which have animated a series of popular movements, both to criticize established institutions and to defend schemes for constructive change. Surely, we know of no anarchist who has celebrated chaos. (1966, 3)

Rather it is the chaos of the capitalist market and statist forms of punishment targeting working class communities of the exploited and oppressed that have so troubled anarchists and mobilized their organizing energies.

Yes, anarchism is eminently practical. Indeed, it finds its inspiration and is rooted in everyday practices of mutual aid and solidarity by which humans have cared for one another and seeks to expand those practices so that they flourish in all spheres of human social life. Emma Goldman addresses the issue of practicality in a poetic passage of her essay "Anarchism: What It Really Stands For." Goldman suggests that the context for assessing practicality must be rethought. In that work she writes:

> A practical scheme, says Oscar Wilde, is either one already in existence, or a scheme that could be carried out under the existing conditions; but it is exactly the existing conditions that one objects to, and any scheme that could accept these conditions is wrong and foolish. The true criterion of the practical, therefore, is not whether the latter can keep intact the wrong or foolish; rather it is whether the scheme has vitality enough to leave the stagnant waters of the old, and build, as well as sustain, new life. In light of this conception, Anarchism is indeed practical. More than any other idea, it is helping to do away with the wrong and foolish; more than any other idea, it is helping to do away with the wrong and foolish; more than any other idea, it is building and sustaining new life. (1969, 49)

Foregoing reforms, critics contend, leaves anarchists only with symbolic violence. Yet for anarchists, there are a quite wide range of activities left to social actors, beyond the rather disappointing options of parliament or projectile.

Anarchist writers and organizers have been generally consistent in claiming that voluntary forms of order and organization are already apparent all around us in the here and now of everyday life. They do not require a revolution to bring them into being. Indeed, many would suggest that a revolution is not possible in their absence (see Shantz 2010). Anarchists note that for many people in the US and Canada survival would be difficult or impossible without the presence of these various sources of mutual aid, from free clinics to clothing and food shares to rent banks, in their lives. Even more, anarchism suggests that the real problem is that statist or archic institutions and organizations prevent these voluntary associations from operating most efficiently, effectively, and freely. Even more, where they do come to pose an open challenge to statist or capitalist rule—as some unions, farming cooperatives, and community defense groups have—at that point the state will mobilize to oppose, constrain, or demolish them, as all of the above noted examples have experienced. One can mention the police assaults upon the MOVE housing complex in Philadelphia and the Black Panther Party community programs as specific examples in the US.

When government is in crisis, declines, or is suspended or abolished, even more forms of informal organization will emerge to meet peoples' needs. Such has been the case during periods of crisis or natural disaster. Amazing examples of mutual aid and direct care can be seen in instances like post-Katrina New Orleans (see Crow 2011). It has also been true during periods of revolutionary upheaval—in the Russian and Spanish Revolutions as well as during the Arab Spring of 2011.

As Krimerman and Perry suggest: "Indeed, government itself is usually blamed for the very chaos which seems to necessitate authority" (1966, 3). Anarchy is "a position which has itself sought the meaning of order and disorder" (1966, 3). Anarchists do not believe the arguments that states are necessary for the maintenance of order. As Goldman sneers: "Unless it be the order of Warsaw after the slaughter of thousands of people, it is difficult to ascribe to governments any capacity for order or social harmony" (1969, 59). Anarchism has never simply been a rejection of politics. It has offered a well-rounded and robust theory (or sets of theories) of human social relations and behaviors. For anarchists, anarchy simply refers to social organization without any constituted external authority.

Goldman suggests that real social harmony only grows out of a shared solidarity of interests. In the words of Proudhon, liberty is the mother not the daughter of order. For Paul Goodman, freedom is *"the condition of initiating activity"* (1966, 55). This is a positive rather than negative conception which focuses on freedom *to* create, the freedom *from* interference. The sense of freedom as initiative and construction has diminished under developed capitalism. The words of Paul Goodman in the middle of the twentieth century still ring, in many ways, true in the first decades of the twenty-first century. According to Goodman:

> For now we are in the age of organized affluence, of automatic technology, feudal monopoly, and symbolic democracy; and the universally prevalent ideology is that Nothing Can Be Done. Therefore, naturally, "freedom" no longer has anything to do with ongoing initiation; it has become the protection of cowering individuals. Such freedom leads to fascism. (1966, 56)

Yet, anarchist impulses within the alternative globalization and Occupy movements have filled many with a powerful sense that something *can be done*. And it can be done in a way that is horizontally rather than vertically organized, participatory rather than passive, and directly active rather than symbolic or representational.

This has profound consequences, not only for action, but for perceiving action, particularly action for change. As Goodman notes, with some disappointment: "The thought that the quality of life is improvable, which was the dogma of liberalism, is now felt by the cowering individual as a threat of tyranny" (1966, 56). Still, this is perhaps as true during the period of the "war on terror" and the crisis of markets as it has ever been. One task of anarchism is "to build up a disobedient and unreliable public" (*Anarchy* 1966, 121).

Human societies on a day to day basis, and in important matters, show the unnecessary nature of state organization. Still there are real questions about how the state might be fully superseded or replaced. There are also important questions about how these new relations might be extended. Government prevents the emergence and ascendance of beneficial alternatives while legitimizing harmful institutions that exist in their place (Krimerman and Perry 1966, 240).

## 4      The Disobedients: Organizing Alternatives, Not Consent

Anarchist strategy involves showing that government does not rest on consent of the governed. As a consequence of rejecting the notion that government rests on consent, anarchists suggest that government abuses are not accidental mistakes but fundamental features of the system of government practice. They are instances of tyranny (Spooner 1966, 242). Anarchists are sharp critics of notions of social contract, as put forward by proponents of liberal democracy, both in their theory and in their practice.

In *On the Social Contract*, French philosopher Jean-Jacques Rousseau argues that the alternative to the defective political influences that give rise to injustice within human societies is a voluntary civil society founded upon unanimous consent to authority, or the general will. This consent forms the basis for governance.

Consent is rarely sought by governments and more rarely given, even by small numbers of people. The population is not consulted on legislation or policy except through the inefficient means of opinion polls. Direct consultation does not occur. Those who disagree with policy, or who would prefer to withhold taxes (in opposition to military expenditures, for example) have few options and are typically met with forms of repression, such as fines, arrests, or imprisonment.

The person subjected to a government they do not want or to which they do not consent is unfree. For the individualist anarchist Lysander Spooner, the difference between this condition of unfreedom and slavery is one of degree only. In his view, there is not a difference in principle between political and chattel slavery. According to Spooner:

> The former, no less than the latter, denies a man's ownership of himself and the products of his labor; and asserts that other men may own him, and dispose of him and his property, for their uses, and at their pleasure. (1966, 243)

For all governments the assertion holds: "Our power is our right" (Spooner 1966, 244). For anarchists, governments are sustained only by force and fraud. Anarchists have no time for the sort of social order promised by states. As Goldman suggests:

> Order derived through submission and maintained by terror is not much of a safe guaranty; yet that is the only 'order' that governments have ever maintained. (1969, 59)

Anarchists reject majority as well as minority rule. In the words of Lysander Spooner:

Majorities and minorities cannot rightfully be taken at all into account in deciding questions of justice. And all talk about them, in matters of government is mere absurdity...To say that majorities, as such, have a right to rule minorities, is equivalent to saying that minorities have, and ought to have, no rights, except such as majorities please to allow them. (1966, 244)

Even where majorities support a government it proves nothing. For Spooner, the only proof provided by majority rule is the potency of government:

Nothing but the tyranny and corruption of the very governments that have reduced so large portions of the people to their present ignorance, servility, degradation, and corruption; an ignorance, servility, degradation, and corruption that are best illustrated in the simple fact that they *do* sustain the governments that have so oppressed, degraded, and corrupted them. (1966, 244–245)

Neither does it suggest that the disapproving minority should also be subjected to government rule. If consent is a sound principle, it is sound for one or two as for thousands.

As far as the question of treason is concerned, some today would suggest that acts of protest or uprising are acts of treason. Yet if no consent to rule is given, how can protest or opposition be treason? For Spooner:

Clearly this individual consent is indispensable to the idea of treason; for if a man has never consented or agreed to support a government, he breaks no faith in refusing to support it. And if he makes war upon it, he does so as an open enemy, and not as a traitor—that is, as a betrayer, or treacherous friend. (1966, 246)

The situation of government tyranny compels people to accept the ballot as a means to shift tyranny to others. Spooner explains the perverse distortion of social interaction among individuals through the ballot, and the opportunism spurred by government rule, as follows:

He sees further that, if he will but use the ballot himself, he has some chance of relieving himself from this tyranny of others, by subjecting them to his own. In short, he finds himself, without his consent, so situated that, if he use the ballot, he may become a master; if he does not use it, he must become a slave. And he has no alternative than these two. In self-defense, he attempts the former. (1966, 249)

Left with no other choice, people may see the ballot as an opportunity—indeed, as the only opportunity. This does not mean it is a desired or satisfactory option. It is not one that is actively chosen from a range of available alternatives. According to Spooner:

> Doubtless the most miserable of men, under the most oppressive government in the world, if allowed the ballot, would use it, if they could see any chance of thereby ameliorating their condition. But it would not therefore be a legitimate inference that the government itself, that crushes them, was one which they had voluntarily set up, or ever consented to. (1966, 249)

In the present period of anti-terror justified state clampdowns on alternative globalization protests, the right of governments to suppress uprisings and criminalize dissent is assumed by many—even among the working classes and poor. But consent is not actively solicited.

Governments depend for survival on the lack of organization of the population and its general apathy or incapacity to contest government or show the absence of consent. Thus anarchists must make real and available other material alternatives. They must work to provide active means for showing the absence of consent among the population and making the refusal of nonconsensual relations possible. Liberating social relations and institutions and establishing new ones requires some form of organization. Anarchism has long put forward a variety of constructive alternatives. For Spooner the choice is rather stark:

> No middle ground is possible on this subject. Either "taxation without consent is robbery," or it is not. If it is *not*, then any number of men, who choose, may at any time associate; call themselves a government; assume absolute authority over all weaker than themselves; plunder them at will; and kill them if they resist. If, on the other hand, "taxation without consent *is* robbery," it necessarily follows that every man who has not consented to be taxed, has the same natural right to defend his property against a tax-gatherer, that he has to defend it against a highwayman. (1966, 250)

In this sense all government is, as Emerson suggested, tyranny. All government rests not on consent but on coercion and all government seeks the subordination of the individual. One can see the nature of statist "freedom" in the response of states to movements for liberty. The final answer is always violence. Of course a vast apparatus of techniques is deployed on a daily basis before the need to resort to that final answer is most pressing. As Goldman notes:

> The only way organized authority meets this grave situation is by extending still greater privileges to those who have already monopolized the earth, and by still further enslaving the disinherited masses. Thus the entire arsenal of government—laws, police, soldiers, the courts, legislatures, prisons—is strenuously engaged in "harmonizing" the most antagonistic elements in society. (1969, 59)

## 5     Conclusion

The presentation of anarchism as purely negative, and the reduction of anarchism to a few crass caricatures has meant that anarchists have had to spend an inordinate amount of time explaining (and re-explaining) the basics of anarchist theory and practice (over and over again). This task of explanatory self-defense has fallen to anarchists perhaps more than for proponents of any other political philosophy. This task has been taken up from the need both to address skeptics and opponents and to correct the, often intentionally, incorrect portrayals that are commonly made of anarchism. As Krimerman and Perry (1966) point out there are probably too many anarchist publications—ranging from stapled, self-produced zines to full books—with titles something along the lines of "What is Anarchism?"

While anarchists have been forced by circumstances to dwell on developing clear and direct introductions, again perhaps as no other political philosophy has been required—even Marxism which is at least familiar to statist thinking—this has meant that fuller and more detailed accounts of anarchist proposals and projects have been less available.

This has thankfully changed somewhat more recently. Since the anarchist upsurge, especially as part of the alternative globalization struggles since Seattle in 1999 and, more recently within the Occupy movements—and encouraged partly by the emergence of a growing anarchist academic wing—there have emerged a variety of more developed discussions of anarchist theory at least. There has also been a re-emergence (perhaps accounting for much of the growth of academic anarchism) of anarchist historiography. Indeed, most of the new anarchist writings have focused on reappraisals of anarchist classics, early theorists and political movements (particularly in Europe during the early twentieth century).

Still, even now, there have been relatively few engaged and detailed treatments of *contemporary* anarchist politics (strategies, tactics, visions, and projects). Perhaps no aspect of contemporary anarchism has received less attention than anarchist approaches to organization and political mobilization. How do contemporary anarchists organize to develop and share resources, devise campaigns, educate themselves and others, and meet the day to day and longer term needs of active political and social movements. Even more, how do anarchists make themselves relevant—and appreciated—resources in the lives of people dealing with the everyday realities of life, including experiences of oppression, deprivation, poverty, and exploitation, in state capitalist societies.

Here again the popular myths and disparaging caricatures remain. Anarchist organization? What an oxymoron. Yet a close look at contemporary anarchist movements reveals a vibrant and compelling range of organizations, and organizational practices, and a complex variety of anarchist organizational visions and practices. Far from being a limited and narrow social perspective based on a similarly limited and narrow view of human nature—in which humans are unproblematically viewed as benign and agreeable—anarchists have developed various perspectives on human activity. Most of these perspectives speak to the complexity and, indeed, *social* character of human nature(s).

Quite apart from being the negative philosophy some have proposed, anarchism has offered, and continues to offer, richly constructive visions and activities, seeing the reorganization of social life in regular, everyday practices by which regular folks care for one another, support each other, and sustain their communities. Anarchism has also offered a range of positive real world practices through which people try to organize and sustain their lives on the basis of self-determination and autonomy from the state and capital.

Despite the stereotypes anarchism offers serious models of organization. Anarchists organize themselves in a variety of ways—from small-scale affinity groups and reading circles to mid-level infoshops and collectives through to larger scale unions and federations that organize and operate across national boundaries and are multinational in scope and operation.

Indeed, in the internet age, even the smaller scale groups often expand beyond the more traditionally anarchist face to face realms to maintain connections, interactions, strategizing, and mobilization internationally. Of course, anarchists have always been internationalists. From involvement in the earliest days of the founding of the First International through international mobilizations in support of the anti-fascist forces during the Spanish Revolution in the 1930s up to the alternative globalization and Occupy movements of the present day, anarchists have sought to transcend national boundaries to organize against states and capital.

Anarchists have engaged in great debates and stirred major controversies over questions of organization and order, liberty and authority. Anarchists have rarely indulged in utopian flights of fancy. They have preferred not to defer the new world to some distant time in the future, choosing instead to act as if the revolution is possible today. More often they have pursued specific projects and activities that, in their view, open or sustain routes to re-invigorate social relations.

Emma Goldman has this to say on the matter of practical anarchy:

> As to methods. Anarchism is not, as some may suppose, a theory of the future to be realized through divine inspiration. It is a living force in the affairs of our life, constantly creating new conditions. The methods of Anarchism therefore do not comprise an iron-clad program to be carried out under all circumstances. Methods must grow out of the economic needs of each place and clime, and of the intellectual and temperamental requirements of the individual. (1969, 63)

As Goldman argues:

> Anarchism does not stand for military drill and uniformity; it does, however, stand for the spirit of revolt, in whatever form, against everything that hinders human growth. All Anarchists agree in that, as they also agree in their opposition to the political machinery as a means of bringing about the great social change. (1969, 63)

Contemporary anarchists have learned the lessons of postmodern times and lack the revolutionary optimism and certitude that marked earlier generations of socialists. They are wary of universal solutions and general panaceas. Yet this does not mean a turn away from key issues and analyses that animated previous generations of anti-capitalist organizers and movements. As one example, workers control and autonomy are necessities in the current period and anarchists see putting demands for workers self-determination on the agenda as a key task. These and other approaches are addressed in specific ways in the chapters that follow.

CHAPTER 2

# Anarchist Tendencies

Some suggest that the essence of anarchism is the commitment to the freedom of the individual (Novak 2010). The famed anarchist orator Emma Goldman, "Red Emma," offers a succinct overview of the anarchist impulse. In her words:

> Anarchism, then, really stands for the liberation of the human mind from the dominion of religion; the liberation of the human body from the dominion of property; liberation from the shackles and restraint of government. Anarchism stands for a social order based on the free grouping of individuals for the purpose of producing real social wealth; an order that will guarantee to every human being free access to the earth and full enjoyment of the necessities of life, according to individual desires, tastes, and inclinations.
>
> GOLDMAN 1969, 62

While explicitly self-identified anarchist movements have emerged in the last two centuries, the revolt at the heart of anarchy has much earlier origins. Indeed, many would suggest that there has been revolt and opposition wherever governments and states have been present within society. In the realm of ideas, historians of anarchism suggest that themes and perspectives that would become central to anarchism can be found prominently within Taoism. Others point to the Stoicism of Zeno of Citium (336–264 BC) and opposition to Plato's vision (see Marshall 1993). Some point later to the works of Rabelais and de la Boétie as precursors to anarchist philosophy (Krimerman and Perry 1966, 7; Marshall 1993).

Organized precursors include some of the Christian sects, such as Anabaptists and Quakers. Some locate anarchist expressions in the Diggers of the English Revolution and the sans culottes of the French Revolution. Others, anthropologists by training, suggest that oppositional forces always emerge, often in violent form, even within stateless societies in moments when concentrations of elite power begin to coalesce or emerge—when some community members organize in a way that suggests the emergence of a proto-state (see Clastres 1989, 2010; Scott 2010).

Goodman outlines some ideals and concerns of social revolution as he sees it from an anarchist perspective. For Goodman:

humane labor, physical security and freedom, mutual aid; and among more thoughtful revolutionaries, the humanizing of technology and the ethical measure of production and consumption. These social ideals are simple and integral, not an amalgam. (1977, 6–7)

Yet, from this there are widely varying positions on how a society or social relations that maintain individual freedom might be secured—and how the transition from unfree social relations to free might be achieved.


## 1      Anarchisms Plural?

By the last years of the nineteenth century, only decades after Proudhon coined the term that would name the political movement, there was already a sense that there might actually be two anarchisms rather than one. On one hand has been a philosophical or individualist tendency in anarchism which has emphasized individual liberty or freedom of the person. The individualist approach has preferred forms of organizing that allow for creative personal expressions and actions. Not surprisingly it has been favored by artists, poets, and writers. On the other hand has been a collective or communist tendency within anarchism which seeks to transform social relations broadly with concerns for equality and collective freedoms.

Given the reality that all forms or tendencies within anarchism have organized in various ways, even if atypical, a book about anarchist organizing should recognize and appreciate differences but not be one that gets hung up detailing differences in anarchist perspectives or, what so often follows, seeks to identify or argue for a true or real anarchism based on a particular tendency's claims about organization.

On the matter of focusing on divisions within anarchism or claims to a "true" anarchism it is best to be cautious. As Krimerman and Perry suggest:

> There is some danger in drawing lines more hard and fast than they actually are and ignoring the agreement that gives substance to anarchism. Further, so simple an endeavor loses sight of a more intriguing question: what issues meant so much as to cause these rebels to erect a forum for debate within their own movement. (1966, 4)

At the same time some notable differences do exist and have shaped significant debates within anarchist movements and projects. These can be touched upon here.

Individualist anarchism has found its greatest favor among petit bourgeois, or middle strata, audiences. It has appealed historically to the shopkeepers, artisanal craftspeople, and small landholders. In the contemporary period it finds resonance among some of the anarchists who run infoshops and bookstores or run anarchist presses or distribution networks. Beyond that its appeal is largely intellectual and its main adherents are among those in the academy. A range of academics have kept the message of individualist anarchism and mutualism alive in books produced largely for academic audiences.

Some collective anarchists have attempted to assert that individualist anarchists are not really anarchists because they supposedly reject the necessity of broad social organization in effecting social transformation. Conversely, many individual anarchists have accused collective or communist anarchists of being fake or pseudo-anarchists simply because they seek broad social organization, particularly involving working class and poor people. Individualist anarchist Benjamin Tucker referred to individualist anarchy as the genuine anarchy and called communistic anarchy "pseudo-Anarchism" (quoted in Krimerman and Perry 1966, 34). For the individualist critics of anarchist communists, larger scale organization is merely an authoritarian ruse—a way to bring Leninism or Marxist organizing methods in through the back door of anarchism.

Never mind that the earliest proponents of anarchism were involved in the socialist internationals and actively worked to organize working class and poor people into larger scale social groupings that might oppose states and capital. And they did so directly in opposition to Marx and the Marxists and decades before Lenin ever asked "what is to be done?"

Individualist anarchists do tend to turn to past social relations for inspiration. The small property holdings of the independent farmer or artisanal craftsperson provide examples for individualist anarchist practice.

Non-communist anarchists, such as the individualist John Henry MacKay, raise the possibility that communist or collective anarchists may have to choose between their anarchist principles and their constructive projects. In MacKay's view, anarchist communism is something of a contradiction in terms. MacKay suggests that anarchism must eventually choose sides for individualism and against communism. Anarchist communism is, in his view, a foolish attempt "at uniting principles in theory which are practically as different as day and night" (1966, 18). Anarchism is, according to MacKay, a non-class perspective. The working class anarchists who professed anarchist communism, are, in fact, simply not anarchist, for MacKay.

In previous eras it was expected that the differences between individualist and communist anarchists would assert themselves in real world practice as anarchism was brought into the great social struggles at hand and as strategies and tactics were given concrete form (Krimerman and Perry 1966, 35). Yet contemporary anarchist movements have tended to move beyond such divisive ruptures precisely as they have grown in real social struggles and as proposals have been put into practices and gained some force within broader movements.

Indeed the most aggressive, and even nasty, arguments over individualism and communism within North American anarchist circles emerged in the mid and late 1980s and 1990s, a more formative period before the upsurge of anarchist politics in the context of alternative globalization movements since Seattle in 1999.

Much of the explicit anarchist movement recently, even after the upsurge of alternative globalization activities, has been, as Bookchin suggested, largely irrelevant within movements and communities of the working classes and oppressed. It has sought a comfortable existence on the margins, secured within subcultural spaces and practices populated by likeminded people of similar demographic characteristics and cultural preferences (as for punk or hip hop). It has taken up theoretical positions, such as primitivism, that are openly hostile to the working class and equate working people with the industrial "megamachine" that is destroying the planet. It has offered few strategies, tactics, or practices for changing the conditions that wear upon and stifle people.

Goodman does not accept the drop out culture of beats and hippies. In his view their activities and their art are simply conventional. In a prescient passage he suggests that the "on the road" fellows readily become "the organization men" only years later. For Goodman:

> It is necessary to want something in order to be frustrated and angry. They have the theory that to be affectless, not to care, is the ultimate rebellion, but this is a fantasy; for right under the surface, obvious to the trained eye, is burning shame, hurt feelings, fear of impotence, speechless and powerless tantrum, cowering before papa, being rebuffed by mama; and it is these anxieties that dictate their behavior in every crisis. Their behavior is conformity *plus royaliste que le roi*. (1977, 193)

More recently things have changed for the better. Some anarchists have taken up tasks of broader social change and radical mobilizations of resistance to structures and relations of exploitation and oppression.

The majority tendency in explicitly anarchist movements has been anarchist communism. Anarcho-syndicalism, revolutionary unionism, has also been a major force—both historically and in the present period. Anarchist communism expresses the intersection of concerns over individual freedom and social organization. For anarchist communism, the individual is a social creature and can only achieve a full, rounded life in cooperation with others. At the same time, no "society" or social relationships can be free if their participants are not free.

In the earliest years of anarchism, during the nineteenth century, anarchists were organized within the International Working Men's Association up to the split at the Hague Congress in 1872. The Russian, Spanish, Latin American, French, and Bulgarian anarchists were all rooted in working class movements (*Anarchy* 1966, 118; Marshall 1993). Notable figures such as Proudhon, Bakunin, Kropotkin, Malatesta, Rocker, Landauer, Sacco, Vanzetti, Goldman, Durrutti, and Berkman were all connected to working class movements.

Almost from the very beginning, communist anarchism has developed as the largest tendency within anarchism. By 1958, Derry Novak, a professor at McMaster University in Hamilton, Ontario, could confidently claim that anarchist communism was "now practically the only anarchist trend." It traces its roots to Baboeuf and the militant working class of the French Revolution.

As Trupp, the fictional stand-in for the anarchist Johann Most, proclaims in the novel *The Anarchists* by John Henry Mackay:

> Whether a few middle-class liberals have invented a new Anarchism is entirely immaterial to me, and does not interest me any more than any other workingman. As regards Proudhon, to whom comrade Auban again and again refers, he has long ago been disposed of and forgotten even in France, and his place has everywhere been taken by the revolutionary, Communistic Anarchism of the real proletariat. (1966, 23)

Anarchist communists try to focus on those areas in which their actions will be useful and in which they might make a material contribution to social transformation. Notably, unlike individualists who have spent perhaps disproportionate amounts of time trying to write anarchist communists and collective anarchists out of the anarchist circle, anarchist communists have focused more on strategic and tactical shortcomings and gaps in attempts to link individualist anarchism with the concerns of working class and poor peoples' everyday realities.

2      Big Tent or Tactical Unity: Synthesist and Platformist Approaches
       to Organizing

In rough terms anarchists sometimes distinguish approaches to organizing in terms of synthesist approaches that emphasize big tent and inclusive projects and platformist approaches that emphasize theoretical and tactical unity as means to accomplish significant social change. Platformists tend to prioritize evaluation of strengths and weaknesses within class forces and the strategic or tactical significance of targeted organizational strength in specific areas (logistical networks, industrial workplaces, large landlords, border controls and migrant defense, for example) while synthesists are more concerned with building spaces that invite people to learn about anarchy. The distinctions are related to perceptions of the need for concerted work on specific projects of strategic importance (platformists) or on building anarchist perspectives more broadly. These distinctions are not hard and fast and synthesists and platformist work together on specific projects.

The platformist tradition in anarchism emerged following the Russian Revolution through the efforts of a group of Russian and Ukrainian anarchists, notably Nestor Makhno and Ida Mett, in exile who sought to analyze why the anarchists had fared so badly during the revolution in comparison with the Bolsheviks. Their conclusion was that despite their vastly better social and political analysis the anarchists lacked effective organizations.

In order that anarchists not make the same mistake in future generations, the Dielo Truda group wrote a position paper, The Organizational Platform for a General Union of Anarchists, in which they laid out some points that might serve as a guide in developing effective revolutionary organizations. Platformists argue that anarchists should come together on the basis of "theoretical and tactical unity." "Theoretical and tactical unity" speaks to a focused sharing of resources and energies that brings otherwise limited anarchist forces together rather than dissipating our efforts. The anarchist organization is a place to come together to reflect on, revise and advance work being done.

Synthesist anarchism refers to organizing approaches that attempt to bring together anarchists of varying tendencies and perspectives within a single group, federation or project. This is sometimes referred to as "big tent" or "small-a" anarchism. The term is drawn from the critical response to the platformist position of the Dielo Trouda Group by a number of Russian anarchists, including notably Voline. The synthesist opponents of platformism argued for an inclusive anarchist organization that did not seek the theoretical and tactical unity advocated by the platformists.

Much of anarchist activity in North America is synthesist, still fitting the description from Dielo Trouda in 1926:

> local organizations advocating contradictory theories and practices, having no perspectives for the future, nor of a continuity in militant work, and habitually disappearing, hardly leaving the slightest trace behind them.

Many of these short lived projects are based on the 'synthesist' model in which contradictory or incompatible ideas and practices are expected to co-exist.

Many of these ephemeral organizations are built on the synthesist basis that platformists have been and remain critical of. While synthesist approaches can succeed, they do exhibit a tendency to be the "mechanical assembly of individuals" that the platformists suggested. Such groupings work relatively well as long as their level of activity doesn't rise above running a bookstore, infoshop or free school. Unfortunately, even in those cases disastrous rifts emerge when meaningful political questions are broached. A consensus based on not wanting to offend other members or declining controversial work because it threatens collective harmony are too often the default positions of synthesist type groups.

For platformists, it is better for anarchists to bring together a core of committed organizers who have some basis for political and practical agreement than to bring together a broad assortment of anarchists who might have widely divergent views of anarchist theory and practice and little basis for agreement about how to organize or develop projects.

Bringing together a hodgepodge of different anarchists might give a (false) sense of movement size and vitality. However, such an assemblage is likely to fracture and split apart at the first sign of disagreement or tactical impasse. At those moments of crisis or repression or need to act, precisely when unity and organizational strength is necessary, the synthesist anarchist group is likely to fall apart or descend into inaction or tactical paralysis.

The lack of theoretical and tactical unity makes the organization prone to factionalism, competition, envy, resentment, distrust, and suspicion. These tendencies can, in turn, be played upon by opposition forces, such as agents of repression. Anarchist communists seek to organize people around their needs and mobilize their energies in meeting those needs. They work to provide examples to show that people can solve their own problems and address key issues in their lives. They do this through projects rooted in affected communities, often within existing institutions such as unions or anti-poverty groups.

It's important to keep in mind that the platform was only ever intended as a beginning, "as the first step towards rallying libertarian forces." Far from being a fully fleshed out program of action it provides only "the outlines, the skeleton of such a programme." Its authors recognized its many gaps, oversights and inadequate treatments.

More than 75 years after it was written and a decade after the fall of the U.S.S.R. the platform has enjoyed a stunning revival. From Ireland and Lebanon to South Africa and Canada, a number of groups have taken up the platform. At a time when anarchist movements are growing, the platform—which was only ever intended as an outline for action—has provided a useful starting point for anarchists looking "to rally all the militants of the organised anarchist movement." As an active minority within the working class, platformists work to provide a rallying point, through example and ideas, in struggles against capital and the state as well as standing against authoritarian ideologies or practices in working class organizations.

The projects detailed and discussed in this book represent both synthesist and platformist approaches to organizing anarchy. Projects like free spaces and free schools as well as media collectives tend to be more synthesist in orientation. Workplace organizing has tended to come from and emphasize theoretical and tactical unity and the autonomous flying squad in Toronto, for example, was initiated by anarchist engaged in some way or another with platformist ideas and organizing.

## 3    On Affinity

Much of anarchist organizing emphasizes relations of affinity. This is an approach to organizing based on voluntary participation, consent, and trust of participants. It is not an approach based on or even accepting of command structures. All participants are involved in decision making and there are expectations of commitment and accountability to the collective. At the same time participants can elect not to participate in specific actions if they cannot give consent.

Even the arch individualist, and prominent influence on philosophical anarchism, Max Stirner, saw the individual acting in organization or association with other self-determining individuals or egoists. Stirner called for a union of egoists. Such an association would be entered freely, of course, as the individual egoist needed to pursue specific aims or interests. They would enter and leave as they saw fit and there would be no contracts, expectations, commitments, obligations, or duties regarding future behavior or interaction.

In my view the union of egoists bears significant resemblance to the affinity groups long advocated by anarchists. Affinity groups have played important parts in organizing within alternative globalization movements and Occupy actions.

Affinity groups are freely engaged, voluntary groupings that people enter into typically to pursue specific tasks or reach specific goals, such as squatting a building or blockading a road. Often affinity groups have provided the basis for political organization during direct actions and protests. Affinity groups are formed on the basis of trust and commitment among members. This makes

the affinity group form particularly suitable for involvement in potentially illegal acts or acts that are likely to lead to criminalization, as in the case of direct actions.

Affinity groups also offer an important counter-weight or bulwark against
social tendencies to avoid responsibility in the pursuit of enjoyment. Affinity
contributes to conditions that support and ethics of responsibility, accountability, and commitment. They are based on deep sentiments of trust, loyalty,
duty, and reliability. In a sense they offer a close peer group—one that can ex-
ert a certain amount of "peer pressure" on members. They also, as importantly,
fulfill human needs and desires for security and a sense of social power.

The emphasis on face to face decision making and affinity relates to broader
understandings of social power and social change for anarchists. As Paul Goodman suggests: "The say of a neighborhood in its destiny can be meaningful
only if the neighborhood has begun to be conscious of itself as a community.
For this, mere 'consent' or 'participation' is not enough; there must be a measure
of real initiating and deciding, grounded in acquaintance and trust" (1966, 382).
For anarchists this comes in part through practices of affinity based organizing
where people build trust and accountability through self-directed, self-determined actions.

4       De-centralism

The anarchist preference for direct decision making and participatory action is
not only reflected in the emphasis on affinity in organizing. It is also expressed
through a commitment to decentralism and decentralizing practices with organizing. This is counter to forms of centralist organization and decision making that predominate within many activist organizations, from community
groups to labor unions.

In centralized systems, Goodman suggests, persons are rendered personnel.
The function of the centralized system is to achieve the goal of the organization rather than the goals of the people or communities involved (1966, 379).
Authority is top-down and decisions, made at headquarters, are passed down-
ward through the chain of command. As Goodman notes: "The system was
designed for disciplining armies, for bureaucratic record-keeping and tax-
collection and for certain kinds of mass-production. It has now pervaded every
field" (1966, 379). Goodman's analysis of bureaucracy is similar to that of the
sociologist Max Weber, yet Goodman emphasizes the limits and dangers of the
system rather than possible efficiencies.

Notably, the system that pervades in government and business is also taken up in non-governmental organizations (NGOs) and activist groups, particularly Greenpeace and the Council of Canadians. It has also been developed as the organizational approach of choice within working class organizations such as labor unions. In these organizations, as in business corporations, activists and organizers have been converted from people to personnel.

Within decentralized practices, people are directly involved in creating and carrying out the functions they perform (Goodman 1966, 379). The organization is simply the manner in which people cooperate. Within decentralized practices there are multiple centers of decision-making. Authority is shifted away from "the top" and ideas are developed and implemented in horizontal practices of face to face interaction and discussion. Each person has the opportunity to be aware of, and direct, the operation(s) of the whole.

Even Marxists have objected to and opposed decentralism and local, face to face decision-making as archaic village (rather than industrial) practice. For anarchists, voluntary association in decentralized groupings has yielded most of human social development (Goodman 1966, 380). For Goodman, anarchists have a dual task: "We need to revive both peasant self-reliance and the democratic power of professional and technical guilds" (1966, 380). So there is no evolutionary assessment of organization forms.

In the view of anarchists, centralism is exploiting and inefficient. It discourages initiative and as a result is wasteful of human cognitive labor. Even the advanced guard of the contemporary tech economies have recognized this and have formed decentralist practices as the basis of their product development. Of course, they maintain centralist practices in terms of corporate decision making and profit flow.

Decentralists do not put undo faith in human nature. Rather, it is because people are fallible that it is crucial to ensure that power is not concentrated in too few hands. For Goodman: "The moral question is not whether men are 'good enough' for a type of social organization, but whether the type of organization is useful to develop the potentialities of intelligence, grace, and freedom in men" (1966, 383). This question animates much of anarchist consideration of organizational forms and practices.

## 5    Direct Action

The emphasis on directness also carries through anarchist approaches to tactics for social change and for confrontation with instituted authorities. Anarchists generally eschew politics of dissent or demand, which seek change through moral appeals to authority or protests against abuses of authority. Instead of dissent or protest anarchists prefer direct action to secure the needs of people affected by the activities of political or economic elites.

There is an important, even crucial, distinction to be made between direct action and protest. Much of activist activity is oriented toward and conceived of in relation to protest or expressions of dissent. Protest is focused on raising concerns to powerholders in a way that seeks to shame them to change or convince them of the wrongness of a course of action in hopes that they will change. It assumes the rationality of political process and the willingness of powerholders to address the needs and concerns of the public. It is a politics of request. It is also in its way an authoritarian politics that privileges the choices and actions of powerholders in granting social change.

Direct action on the other hand privileges the needs and self-activity of non-elites and non-authorities. It is not geared toward shaming powerholders, who have no shame, or making requests upon them that they will, hopefully, possibly deliver on. Rather direct action asserts and affirms the capacities of people to determine their own affairs and to act in ways that directly secure their needs and interests (rather than relying on the good graces of the authorities). Direct action affirms that people can determine their own needs and develop mechanisms for achieving them. At the same time, in the face of harmful activities by state and capital, direct action asserts that the people harmed have no obligation to accept that harm or pursue only those mechanisms approved by powerholders for ending that harm. Thus if a company or state is undertaking a project that is threatening a community the best response may well be sabotage to directly and unequivocally end that project rather than the appeals of protesters asking those who benefit the project to halt it.

As Emma Goldman suggests:

> Anarchism therefore stands for direct action, the open defiance of, and resistance to, all laws and restrictions, economic, social and moral. (1969, 65)

Anarchists pursue practices of direct action in all economic, political, and cultural realms. As Goldman puts it: "Direct action against the authority in the shop, direct action against the authority of the law, direct action against the invasive, meddlesome authority of our moral code, is the logical, consistent method of Anarchism. Will it not lead to a revolution? Indeed, it will" (1969, 67). Again the potentiality for self-directed action to achieve gains and develop practical, experiential capacities for self-determination are stressed.

## 6    Against Majoritarianism in Politics

Anarchists place little trust in majoritarianism. Indeed, they view it as one of the potential threats to liberty and innovation. Majoritarianism reflects the dominance of quantity over quality. This is not surprising in a socio-economic context in which exchange value supercedes use value in virtually all matters of social interchange, not only in the realm of economics. As Goldman notes with dissatisfaction: "Our entire life—production, politics, and education—rests on quantity, on numbers" (1969, 69). This reflects a social system based on measures and accounting of values.

The reduction of politics to quantity is expressed in the twenty-first century era of neo-liberal capitalism as in perhaps no other period in human history. The dominance of various public opinion polls, presented in an almost obsessive manner on almost any public matter, of large or small significance is a hallmark of political discourse in contemporary liberal democracies. Public opinion polls have come to be what Emma Goldman has called "the omnipresent tyrant" (1969, 73). Typically the poll results are presented without any political context or meaningful analysis—a signal of the subsumption of quality to quantity. Beyond polls one might also look at the use of first part the post political arrangements that allow political parties to claim victory with only a small percentage of votes in their favor. In many recent elections in the US and Canada, for example, parties have seized power on the basis of "support" from barely 20 percent of the eligible voter pool. Indeed, it is well recognized that the overwhelming focus on quantity, rather than the quality of people's involvement in matters of civic interaction and decision making plays a very large part in discouraging participation in elections. People view the process as ineffectual and alienating, allowing for now real improvement in their lives. Notions of voter apathy and cynicism, which the pollsters present as default explanations for low participation rates in elections, mask the fact that many people stay home on election night because they have arrived at an accurate assessment of likelihood that voting will actually improve their lives.

As Goldman has outlined:

> In politics, naught but quantity counts. In proportion to its increase, however, principles, ideals, justice, and uprightness are completely swamped by the array of numbers. In the struggle for supremacy the various political parties outdo each other in trickery, deceit, cunning, and shady machinations, confident that the one who succeeds is sure to be hailed by the majority as the victor. That is the only god,—Success. As to what expense, what terrible cost to character, is of no moment. (1969, 69)

Anarchists are quick to point out that liberty and progress, throughout human history, have often arisen from the minority. But these minorities tend to come from excluded or oppressed majorities within state capitalist societies.


## 7    Individuality

Both individualist and communist anarchists assert the need to develop social relations that appreciate the worth of human individuals beyond their measure in labor or labor value. Anarchist communism is "based upon a socialized form of production and consumption and not upon a specious form of individual independence from the economic forces of humanity—an exploded middle-class fiction still swallowed innocently by many an Anarchist-Individualist" (Senex 1966, 36). Human individuality is always being made and remade in cooperation, consultation, and creation with others.

The individual and society are not competing opposites, as many contemporary neo-liberals would argue, but rather represent components of complementary relationships. To separate them is to speak in ideological abstraction.

During the period of the emergence and consolidation of sociology as an academic discipline, social thought was dominated by political liberalism and *laissez faire* economics. This has been associated with liberalism is the notion of individualism. Associated with liberalism are notions of competitive individualism, particularly of individual competition and "success" through the market. Goldman drew a sharp distinction between her conception of individuality and liberal notions of individualism. In her view, the individualism of liberalism reflected an economic and social agenda of the capitalist market and liberal democratic states. For Goldman: "Rugged individualism has meant all the 'individualism' for the masters, while the people are regimented into a slave caste to serve a handful of self-seeking 'supermen'" (1972, 89). Individuality is based in diversity, while individualism derives its power through the indistinguishable characteristics of atomized individuals as represented through the liberal state and markets (Haaland 1993, 84). Goldman's analysis echoes concerns raised by Tönnies in his discussion of the instrumental relations between people that mark conditions of *Gesellschaft*.

Goldman saw her theory as bringing together the communitarianism of Kropotkin with the individuality of Nietzsche or Ibsen. Goldman sought to address the lasting sociological tension of the relationship between the individual and society. She recognized and sought to understand the interdependence "of social organization and individual well being" (Haaland 1993, 6). She recognized the dangers of mass organization as well as the threat posed by the unfettered, socially irresponsible individual. She did not join the liberals in celebrating the individual uncritically. Neither did she join the Marxists in associating the individual with bourgeois thought and uncritically subsuming concern for the individual into the collective.

Indeed, Goldman and her colleague Max Baginsky issued a statement at the 1907 Anarchist Conference in Amsterdam in which they attempted to rethink relationships between individuality and social structure. They sought to correct "a mistaken notion that organization does not foster individual freedom; that, on the contrary, it means the decay of individuality" (Goldman and Baginsky 1907, 310). The development of individuality is, for Goldman and Baginsky, a "mutual process" that is based in "co-operative effort with other individualities" (1907, 310). Organization requires creative individuality as individuality requires cooperative creativity in production.

For Kropotkin, individuals did not create their world in an atomized fashion. Rather, individuality was realized through their social activity. Goldman was wary of claims such as those made by the communist theorist Alexandra Kollontai that communist morality "demands all for the collective" (1977, 231).

## 8    An Alternative Socialism

Some of the most effective and insightful works of anarchist analysis have involved anarchist criticisms of authoritarian socialism. Anarchism and socialism have emerged and developed in tension, and even open conflict, with each other. Many times they have worked together as allies. At other times, as in Russia and Spain, moving from allies to being challengers and opponents engaged in often violent struggles against one another. The Marxists in the First International, hoping to flee the anarchists, infamously moved the headquarters of the International to New York.

One of the key contributions of anarchism has been to pose questions about what socialism might really mean and how it might properly be achieved. Some anarchists, particularly individualists, have been harsh in their rejection of socialism. Others see anarchism as part of socialist history more broadly conceived and focus condemnation on authoritarian manifestations within the tradition.

In organizational terms, anarchist criticisms of socialism focus on the rejection of notions of state power and seizure of state authority. Anarchists do not organize to "take over" state power or the reigns of government. Anarchism differs from state socialism or Marxism in this regard. For anarchists: "Anarchism wants the absence of all government which—even if it abolishes 'class rule'—inevitably separates mankind into two great classes of exploiters and exploited" (MacKay 1966, 20). As a consequence, they also reject political vanguardism and the elitism of party politics geared toward achieving access, whether violently through revolution or gradually through reformist means, to the state. Thus, anarchists oppose Leninist forms of organization through centralized party structures.

The individualist anarchist Benjamin Tucker suggests that anarchism and socialism have the same starting point—the view that labor should possess its own products. From that starting point there is much divergence. How is such a situation of labor control over its products to be secured? The basis of socialism is (as in Adam Smith) the recognition that "the natural wage of labor is its product" (Tucker 1966, 64). This wage, the product, is the only truly just source of income (Tucker 1966, 64).

The exploitation of labor is only possible because it is supported by legal privilege and monopoly. The only way to secure for labor its' just income is to end that legal privilege and monopoly. It is upon the question of how to achieve the end of that legal privilege and monopoly that socialism split, according to Tucker, along the paths of liberty and authority (1966, 64). For Tucker, the real distinction is between principles of liberty and authority. Corresponding to the first is anarchism. Corresponding to the second is state socialism. The conflict between anarchism and socialism, between liberty and authority, are in Tucker's view almost equivalent to the history of human life (1966, 62).

At the start, libertarian sentiments were strong, even within non-anarchist forms of socialism. Tucker traces anarchism and socialism to the same source, though noting their divergence over time, based on the mistaken analysis of the state by authoritarian socialists.

The strong, majority, support for Bakunin in the First International shows the persuasiveness, and positive reception, of anarchist sentiments within the organized socialist movement. Anarchists and socialists shared general commitments to revolution but differed greatly in terms of how they understood revolution and how they saw it being potentially realized.

For anarchists, the traditional organizational structures of the Left are no longer, if they ever were, effective or even suitable for contemporary conditions of struggle. Anarchist organization requires direct involvement, participation, and responsibility. And anarchists try to bring these alive in the real world of everyday life through experiments in various forms of organization.

# CHAPTER 3

# Against the State: Anarchism and the Problems with Social Movement Theories

> Most people regard anarchists as disorderly and unpleasant, but few fear them as instruments of senseless terrorism
>
> CHARLES W. LOMAS (1968, 21)

Sociological theories of social movements have had a consistently tough time with anarchism. Right from the beginning social movement studies have been perplexed by anarchism and anarchist politics. On the one hand this is related to the fact that most social movement studies have understood politics in terms of the state (and access to the state) and prioritized in their studies those movements that have made specific demands or claims upon the state. On the other hand social movement studies, as for much of sociology more broadly, have conceptualized anarchism according to the by now familiar terms of chaos or disorder or, at most, viewed it as a form of individual, personal rebellion. Social movement theories have been ill prepared, and often unmotivated, to come to grips with anarchism as an organized movement (rather than inchoate uproar or rebellion) that seeks the abolition of the state (rather than some accommodation with or seizure of it).

The inability to come to grips with anarchist movements is reflected in part in the curious ways in which anarchist movements (or even more expansively, anarchist approaches to revolution) have been conceptualized and labeled by those researchers who studied and wrote about them. Terms like rebellion, even banditry, are used. Evaluations such as infantile get tossed around. The other source of much difficulty for social movement theories in coming to terms with anarchism is the overwhelming statism of most of the sociological frameworks, and virtually all of the dominant ones. Both of these failings are, in part, related to the acceptance of the modern state, and a periodization of state development, with sociological theories of social movements.

The emphasis on state centered activities has been such that scholars like Hank Johnston suggest the modern state developed in tandem with social movements. Social movements and protest are understood as simply regular politics by other means (Johnston 2011). The term "contentious politics" speaks to the view that social movements represent part of regular politics—though expressed in a novel manner. Movements and protests are viewed as only ac-companiments to or accessories to political parties and elections. Or, in John-ston's words: "Nowadays, people rely not only on political parties and elec-tions" (2011, 1). Social movements are viewed as non-institutional forms of popular pressure and claims of the state. This is a perspective or approach taken by hegemonic social movement scholars like Charles Tilley and Dona-tella della Porta as well.

Jo Freeman and Victoria Johnson (1999), academics with activist experi-ence, focus on waves of protest, as in the 1930s and 1960s, but here too the framework is one of movement transformations within existing state struc-tures. Outcomes are measured in policies and priorities as well new institu-tions or interest groups but predominantly as reforms. Movements are seen as reaffirming values such as equal rights or personal dignity (1999, x). Johnston suggests that the targets of social movements "are usually state authorities who are in positions to make changes and reforms that answer protesters' demands" (2011, 1). Johnston only allows it as "possible that protesters sometimes chal-lenge nonstate institutions" (2011, 1).

Yet anarchists are as likely to target non-state institutions (landlords, bosses, gentrifying developers, poor bashing businesses, etc.) as state institutions. And it is precisely because they can win important, real concessions or outright capitulation on a direct local (or broader) level from such immediate targets that cannot be won as readily (or meaningfully) from state bureaucracies. And it is also because they do not seek primarily managed reforms or modest changes. Rather they seek the fulfillment of participants' needs (as determined by participants, not by authorities).

Neither do anarchists seek recognition for novel identities or cultural prac-tices in the manner assumed by new social movement theories. Anarchists do not seek acceptance or tolerance for identities or cultures within a statist framework (*a la* multiculturalism or diversity policies). Rather they express a cultural autonomy that emphasizes self-determining practices and relations that break dependence on (or defining by) that state. Anarchists have never bought into the "presumption of responsiveness of elected officials to those they govern" (Johnston 2011, 2). Neither do they seek nor accept the paternalis-tic actions of government officials in making crucial decisions about peoples' lives and interests.

For social movement theorists such approaches are arbitrarily defined as non-movement (or primitive movement) largely because they are said to rep-resent actions of the pre-modern period (before the rise of the nation state). Incredibly, the statist bias in social movement theory is so ingrained as to re-construct the life of humanity in statist terms. Thus Johnston suggests:

Throughout the course of history, the experience of most human beings was not one of freely entering into a contract to form a state, but rather that the state was simply a fact of life. They were born into it with author-ity relations already established, rulers over them who made demands and took taxes. (2011, 4)

Yet as most anthropologists, including anarchist anthropologists like Harold Barclay and David Graeber, point out, it is by now well established that most of human history has, in fact, been lived in the complete absence of states (as, for example, gatherer and hunter communities).

1      Of Modern and Pre-modern

Much of academic social movement theory follows Hobsbawm's schema (sim-ilarly asserted and advanced by Charles Tilley in social movement studies) of pre-modern and modern repertoires. Pre-modern repertoires are said to be lo-cal in focus, limited in duration, and directly and immediately (and unmediat-edly) active against specific targets (economic and political). This schema leads many social movement theorists to overlook actions, *still* undertaken by movements, such as direct actions against local (or national or global in cases like alternative globalization movements) authorities.

This draws upon the earlier work of Hobsbawm (1959) and his notion of "primitive protests." Part of Hobsbawm's argument suggests that protest was primitive because it occurred in periods of limited state capacity. It was not directed *to* the state for accommodation *from* the state. Theorists in this view, such as Johnston, suggest that these cannot even be counted as social move-ments. Largely because the modern state did not exist. Johnston is quite ex-plicit. He states that "social movements always occur in the context of the state...the two must be considered together" (2011, 16). Johnston really means, as do most in the sociological traditions of social movement studies, that social movements are merely "noninstitutional means of making claims or amelio-rating grievances" via the state (2011, 16). For Johnston: "This means that today social movements target mostly the state to affect policy relevant to members' interests" (2011, 11).

Influenced by functionalist notions of the day, Chalmers Johnson identifies anarchism as something of a dysfunction, the result of an inappropriate or in-sufficient approach to simple change (i.e. reformist or gradual change) (1964, 7). That is, anarchism is marked as a failing of simple change rather than a "func-tional" response to social problems in its own right. Johnson, adopting the pre-/modern view even identifies anarchist rebellion as "nostalgic" (1964, 40). Anarchist movements are, according to Johnson, an attempt to relieve dysfunctions caused by other attempts to relieve dysfunctions (1964, 40). He offers an example of rebellion against industrialization (and the strengthening of state power that accompanies it).

Anarchists are identified as those groups left out of the broader conflict between bourgeoisie and proletariat—peasants, artisans, and those "bypassed by history" (1964, 40). Yet this conveniently ignores the fact that anarchism emerges as part of the international working class movements and was, for a time, the dominant or leading tendency within it. For Chalmers Johnson, the ideology of anarchism reflects the view of the obsolete or threatened. Anarchists supposedly articulate a future based in visions of an idealized but redundant past (1964, 41). They are à la Hobsbawm (through to Tilly) primitive or premodern rebels. In a manner foreshadowing Hank Johnston, Chalmers Johnson suggests: "Empirically such revolutions are launched in order to counteract a change from pre-national community to national community" (1964, 42).

Johnson offers the example of the Spanish Revolution but seems completely oblivious to the anarcho-syndicalism of the revolution in regions like Catalonia and the large scale industrial reorganization in Barcelona along anarchist lines (production, transportation, education, media, health care, etc.). Johnson provides a clear statement of the view that anarchism is a primitive or infantile movement. In his view anarchism is an immature political philosophy in a particular sequence of radicalization. As he states:

> An individual relatively aware of the sources of dysfunction afflicting the system of which he is a member may adopt an anarchistic ideology at an early stage of his political consciousness. Later he may switch to a socialist or to a communist position.
>
> JOHNSON 1964, 44

The political maturity supposedly comes with a recognition of the permanency (and legitimacy and desirability?) of the state. This is a position shared by liberals and many communists alike.

Yet contemporary activists (and activist-scholars) do not subscribe to such schema. Anarchists and non-anarchists alike, movement activists take a much more diverse and inclusive view of movement activity. Direct action and tactics and strategies of autonomy and self-determination are little understood, or even recognized, within some social movement theories. Where they are acknowledged there is an effort to constrain them within the bounds of pre-established movement characteristics. So property damage or sabotage are viewed as "extremist" acts (in a way that reproduces repressive state designations) geared toward publicity or attention getting or public displays of dedication or commitment. For activists, however such acts are often understood as necessary and reasonable efforts to *stop* or derail harmful and destructive actions directly and immediately (rather than as appeals to the state or business to do it).

Indeed the designation of social movements as *modern* forms of protest is itself problematic (as is the whole pre-modern and modern bifurcation of protest). Perhaps it makes more sense to speak of resistance. So-called modern movements draw on and deploy a range of practices, strategies, and tactics of the supposedly pre-modern protests. This too is a manifestation of the statist assumptions of social movements.

Seizing grains from merchants' storehouses to address food shortages or destroying workhouses in which the poor have been made to labor for local businesses represent forms of unmediated direct action that have contemporary forms (Commando Bouffe food liberation actions at expensive restaurants or high end grocery stores, for example). Other examples include destroying fences raised to enclose common areas (woods, meadows, fields, etc.).

Actions like charivari or rough music—showing up at the house of an offending authority and making loud noises, singing songs, chanting, and/or hurling insults—which contemporary direct action and anarchist groups deploy, are arbitrarily ignored or consigned to a false pre-modern or "primitive" designation. Riots and property damage are similarly consigned in the Hobsbawm-Tilley schema to a pre-modern status and overlooked or misunderstood. And the underlying reason for this is that such actions do not easily fit within the framework that conceptualizes movements as primarily as means for appeals to states.

What does it say that the hyper-modern movements *par excellence* of the twenty-first century largely draw on and display the supposedly pre-modern characteristics? Social movements are not and have not been solely adjuncts to the state.

## 2    On So-Called Agitators

Early accounts of movements focused on the notion of the agitator, particularly the so-called "outside agitator." This figure, through power of speech or appeal of propaganda, is said to spur groups (conceived typically as masses or mobs) to action (with an implication that people may not have engaged in action otherwise, in the absence of the agitator) (D'Arcus 2013). The agitator is viewed as playing the role of trying to incite a riot or induce members of their audience to undertake seditious activity (Lomas 1968, 22). The analysis of the agitator also tends to assume that the primary role of agitation is to encourage more moderate forces to converge to seek a solution (within the existing social order largely). A distinction is drawn between violent agitators and moderates with a social conscience (who are drawn to protest and reform rather than direct action).

By the mid-twentieth century social scientists had accepted that social and political conditions, rather than agitation or irrationalism, were most crucial in the initiation and growth of movements. Yet police and security forces have clung to the agitation thesis.

The notion of agitation, as deployed by nuanced analysts like Charles W. Lomas, is actually more insightful that much of the state-centric social movement literature. Lomas recognizes that the line between nonviolent and violent action is thin and movement violence is typically sparked by police violence (1968, 2). Most movement violence is, in fact, counter-violence in response to actions by authorities (public or private) (see Shantz 2011). Lomas recognizes short range, long range, and revolutionary agitation. He does not exclude actions geared at immediate and attainable local goals (as being premodern, for example). And movements may use any and all of these at various points. Lomas does note that agitation may be aimed at the social order itself rather than simply toward the addressing of grievances or the raising of dissent. This goes beyond the limited approach of much social movement analysis.

The agitator is closely linked to a notion of the professional troublemaker. Note that such a notion is still very much alive in police analyses of anarchism and radical environmental movements, for example, in the contemporary context. Though social movement theorists tend to have moved on from such perspectives, it is by no means a relic of the past. Indeed, the agitator thesis has found proponents among social science analysts in the period of alternative globalization (see Darlington 2006).

Analyses of agitation typically focus on anarchist organizers and anarchist oration. Indeed, the anarchist has been the agitator par excellence in such accounts. It could even be said that the agitation or outside agitator thesis was developed to address anarchism. This is not overly surprising perhaps given the long history of effective anarchist orators, from Mikhail Bakunin through Johan Most and Emma Goldman.

Often early analysts, in agitator or collective behavior approaches held movements and their participants in some disdain. Often the focus was on the psychology of movement involvement or the motives of participants (Cantril 1941). Later, movements became signs of dysfunction. More recent movement theories (post-1970s) have shifted focus to questions of access to resources, organizational forms, opportunity structures, and goals or aims. Connections between collective actions and access to resources have been closely analyzed (Freeman and Johnson 1999, 4).

New social movement theories focus on constructions of meaning, ideology, and culture. New social movement theories shift the emphasis to consciousness or group identity and shared values. Key for their analysis is identification (across locales). However, the emphasis remains on changes within a liberal democratic framework.

## 3    Beyond Protest and Dissent

Note too that even the notion of *protest* preferred by social movement theorists is a limited (statist and reformist) category. Protest—expressions of dissent and disagreement—do not represent the range and variety of oppositional expression (including attempts to stop and replace practices of exploitation, oppression, and repression) or what might better be called simply resistance.

This lays out important assumptions of the social movements perspectives. In addition to the state centrism of social movement theories is the focus on state policy change and reforms. Other aspects of the social movement theories include focus on national politics and conceptions of citizenship and citizenship expansion. For social movement theorists like Johnston:

> a package of tactics emerged, including marches, demonstrations, meetings, strategy sessions, petitions, all conceived as a means to put pressure on politicians to address movement claims, concerns, and grievances. (2011, 13)

Both the listing of movements practices and assumptions about their aims are insufficient or completely misguided when it comes to understanding anarchism.

The limited view of social movement theories is also reflected in their histories of social development. While they tend to touch upon Locke and Hobbes and the social contract, Locke and inalienable rights, Rousseau on democracy and Jefferson on democracy in their telling of the French and American Revolutions they say little of alternative forms of democracy and anarchic

manifestations from the Diggers and Levellers, through Brebeuf, and Proudhon and notions of participatory democracy and mutual aid rather than social
contract (a language of market players anyway).

Social movement theories prefer a liberal pluralistic view of the state that
unhinges the state from class interests and capitalist accumulation regimes.
Thus they expect that social movements can secure a particular configuration
of state institutions that expresses subaltern interests in a predominant way.
For Johnston:

> Protest is a noninstitutional means of making claims or ameliorating
> grievances when state authorities, by limiting, ignoring, or closing off in-
> stitutional channels of access, are not responsive to popular pressure.
> (2011, 16)

In many ways, anarchist movements are like other social movement aggregations. They bring together varied organizations and practices, including informal groups as well as individuals who are not affiliated with anarchist groups
but have interests in anarchist ideas and/or practices. They are often complex
aggregations and they federate or connect through networks typically. Against
the false stereotypes of anarchism, anarchist movements involve planning, deliberation, and coordination as, indeed, do other social movements. Differences often exist between groups and projects and these must be negotiated to
show unity to opponents or authorities, as is the case for all social movements
(Johnston 2011, 14).

Social movement theorists, following Tilly, emphasize movement characteristics (famous WUNC displays) that are geared to better influence decision
makers. This obscures movements that seek capacities to make their own decisions and not rely on authorities to better decide for them. Johnston suggests:

> Members and groups coalesce around an issue or grievance to make their
> demands known publicly, and show their force to representatives of the
> state in order to effect a change. (2011, 14)

Social movement theories also misunderstand expressions of uncivil politics
(Shantz 2011). This is so largely because they view movements through the lens
of appeals to the state or media to "make their voices heard" (Johnston 2011, 15).
It also reflects a lingering misreading of civil rights movements and a singular
focus on civil disobedience narrowly conceptualized. Thus dominant theories
see violence as a response to a lack of members (to show dedication or raise
awareness publicly). Direct action is misunderstood as a means to draw media

attention or compel dialogue. Thus social movement theories have never quite understood tactics like the black bloc or sabotage (Shantz 2011).

Such movements are not about making their voice heard as in social movement theories (see Johnston 2011, 15) but seek to speak for themselves. Anarchists have long argued that ongoing engagement with states and/or prioritization of state interests can lead to social movement organizations coming to look like and act like state organizations.

## 4      Against Representation

Social science based social movement approaches have been framed by what anarchist sociologist Richard Day calls a hegemonic approach. That is, they focus on formal aspects of movement organization geared toward capture of the state (in electoral, rhetorical, or dialogic terms). In contrast to this hegemonic perspective Day suggests that contemporary movements as often (or more often) pursue a politics of affinity. Affinity emphasizes structural issues such as decentralized organization, horizontalism of structure, participatory decision making, and egalitarian social forms. It also emphasizes issues of autonomy and self-determination—and spreading spaces for their realization— rather than appeals to the state for power or redress of grievances.

Social movement theories assume a representational perspective on democracy rather than the participatory and direct approaches preferred by anarchists. The generally liberal approach of social movement theories emphasizes citizen rights and "democratic" representation within parliamentary democratic forms. Even in terms of equality, social movement theorists like Hank Johnston refer to "equality of access to state agents" rather than "economic equality directly" (2011, 19). Anarchists emphasize the latter.

So skewed against anarchism are mainstream social movement theorists that Simon Tormey in his recent book on *The End of Representational Politics* does not include a discussion of anarchist movements that have been crucial motors in driving the end of representational politics in the West. Though he does at least mention Peter Kropotkin.

Recognizing that corporate lobbying skews equality of access they still speak of democracy and look at social movements as means to apply pressure in search of "accountability and responsiveness" (Johnston 2011, 20). This makes clear the liberal emphasis of social movement approaches (and their lack of engagement with critical theories of the state in capitalism). Social movement theorists as part of their liberal, rather than critical, approach tend to posit the state as an almost neutral entity that is simply influenced more heavily by some economic and political elites rather than viewing the state as a distinct structure and institution of rulership, regulation, and accumulation with specific class histories and class character.

Johnston goes so far as to suggest that the capitalist "democratic" state is non-hierarchical and open (2011, 23). Social movement theorists even distinguish between authoritarian and non-authoritarian states (a curious distinction that makes "sense" only in a liberal framework—and none at all from an anarchist one). The state is, if anything, hierarchical and closed (to real, meaningful participation in decision making by regular folks on important issues that affect their lives). It should go without saying that states are by definition authoritarian.

Social movement theories express notions of "the ideal state" (Johnston 2011, 29). For anarchists, of course, there is no ideal state (except perhaps and abolished one).

## 5      Toward Infrastructures of Resistance

Social movement theories tend to offer a bifurcated model of social change. In this model, social change is dichotomized between revolutions or prolonged periods of social rupture on one hand and more momentary protests and grievance expressions on the other. Anarchists tend to emphasize a position somewhere between these two. They mobilize actions beyond protests and grievance raising and seek to build foundations that could sustain struggles and mobilizations over time (possibly contributing to revolutionary transformations but also carrying movements over lean times and down cycles).

While social movement theories have been ill suited to contribute to understandings of anarchist movements (or even to conceptualize them properly)—largely due to the statism of the dominant sociological approaches and the restrictive schema of pre-modern/modern/post-modern—there is one analytical concept with social movement theories, specifically resource mobilization theories, that has much to offer social analysis of radical movements (indeed all movements). This is the notion of infrastructures of dissent. Unfortunately this insight or resource mobilization theory has been marginal within sociological social movement theories, rendered as something of a footnote. I have preferred to develop this notion in terms of infrastructures of resistance, for reasons that should be somewhat clear but which I develop in what follows.

Resource mobilization theories shifted focus to questions of how movements organize themselves and/or how forms of organization influence movement goals and actions (and participant expectations and involvement). Resource mobilization theories have tended to emphasize formal organizations and practices and to downplay spontaneity presenting a mistaken image of movements as outcomes of rational calculations (Freeman and Johnson 1999, 1). They also prioritize formal movement organizations and especially those geared toward accessing political opportunities via the state or formal political realms.

Much of social movements theorizing has missed these insights in relationship to anarchism because, succumbing to stereotypes and caricatures or generally dismissive of anarchism anyway, they mistakenly assume that anarchist movements are unorganized or disorganized. At the same time some anarchists, particularly those of individualist, counter-cultural, insurrectionist orientation (or those who are primarily motivated by academic interests), have eschewed or rejected concerns with questions of infrastructure or durability in movement resources. This insight of resource mobilization theory is based on the little regarded or remarked upon concept of the infrastructures of dissent, a relatively minor footnote in the vast corpus of social movement theories taken as a whole.

Freeman and Johnson note that it is the tension or interplay between spontaneity and structure that marks social movements. Both are present in all social movements regardless of issue or orientation. Collective behavior scholars focus on spontaneous activities as in crowds, panics, riots, or social movements (Freeman and Johnson 1999, 1). Social movements are more organized aspects of these phenomena (Freeman and Johnson 1999, 1).

# CHAPTER 4

# Theory Meet Practice: Evolving Ideas and Actions in Anarchist Free Schools

This chapter examines evolving theoretical perspectives and activities within anarchist free schools situating pedagogical commitments within changing activist engagements. Beginning with a critical discussion of anarchist pedagogical approaches the chapter outlines how anarchists have adapted their efforts through real world organizing over the last two decades. The chapter offers comparative analysis of organizing within two actual free schools and how the interaction of theory and practice as well as state response have transformed these spaces as sites of learning and action. Tensions between class struggle and insurrectionary approaches are examined as are issues of identity and social background. Offering a social history of anarchist struggles against neoliberalism and austerity within the Canadian state context the chapter discusses the importance that issues of decolonization and intersectionality have gained within anarchist pedagogical approaches (and the decolonizing of anarchist pedagogies) more recently compared with free school work in the late 1990s. Connections between anarchist pedagogies and community organizing, especially solidarity with Indigenous communities and anti-poverty movements are addressed.

## 1    Anarchism, Education, and Free Schools

Anarchism has grown dramatically as a part of movements against authoritarianism and inequality, states, and capital over the last two decades. Indeed anarchism has become one of the most important radical movements (in perspective and practice) of the twenty-first century as people seek alternatives to state capitalist austerity in a context in which previously influential alternatives, notably Marxism and social democracy have waned or been exposed as false models.

The development of anarchism has led many to question dominant idea systems and mechanisms by which ideas, perspectives on the world, are constructed and disseminated. This has impelled critical thinking about education and has fueled, and been fueled by, a desire to develop alternative educational practices. At the same time alternative educational venues, initiated and sustained by anarchists have provided important resources in the growth and transformation of anarchist movements more broadly. Among the most significant forms of anarchist real world project have been free schools, collective efforts to engage critical perspectives on the world and to support community organizing materially.

Anarchist playwright Pat Halley once wrote in the pages of the anarchist journal *Fifth Estate* that, "The purpose of education is to kick the animal out of you" (2013, 25). By this Halley made the argument that, for anarchists, formal education in state capitalist societies plays a function of domestication. It works to constrain peoples' desires, autonomy and sense of self-determination while inculcating students with systemic values, respect for instituted authorities, and routinization into daily practices of compliance. This is a process that has been illustrated in detail by social theorists such as Michel Foucault who notes the similarity in structures and practices between schools, prisons, and factories. Each serves to (re)produce ritualized practices of work discipline.

Even more, for Halley and other anarchists, formal education poses the notion that the current order is a natural and essential one. The current system is portrayed further as "the best of all possible worlds," to use the popular phrase. For the *Fifth Estate*:

> In one such as ours, where everything that it means to be human has been grotesquely twisted to the needs of the ruling order, formal education teaches unquestioning respect for authority, acceptance of hierarchies, carrying out tasks that benefit others but harm yourself and the planet, adherence to work in which you have no interest, measurement in abstractions, militarism and nationalism, an inherent value in the production and consumption of commodities, religious mysticism, and perhaps the most insidious, that the current system is the only possible manner in which the world can be constructed.
>
> *Fifth Estate* 2013, 25

Modern schooling, as a formal social institution, was created, and has developed, in the context of industrial state capitalism (Matthews). For anarchists, formal schooling has been made to fit the needs and values prioritized with, and reflective of, capitalist social relations. This includes preparation for work, the acceptance of work for wages, work discipline, management conditioning, and flexibilization. It emphasizes discreet projects over holistic development. Such schooling acts to construct the majority as an exploitable workforce within a specific national state context. It is geared toward the needs of the current economy. It is not so concerned with the development of free and autonomous people in free and autonomous communities (Anonymous 2013).

For education critic Daniel Quinn, much of schooling serves to keep youth out of the job market, thus manipulating unemployment rates. It also serves to keep them off the streets and busy rather than collectively responding to conditions of need and/or anger.

Youth are not taught independent survival skills which they might desire (knowledge of local environments, food sources, production skills). Rather they are left only with the option to work for wages as mediated means to meet some survival needs (and many others geared only toward the survival of the market, such as many consumer goods).

For anarchists, schooling renders children and youth a population to be evaluated, surveilled, controlled, and disciplined (Anonymous 2013, 26). Authorities that stand over them are to be respected. A writer in the student movement pamphlet *En suspense*, a publication of the Quebec student uprisings of 2012, suggests:

> According to several parents practicing home schooling or "unschooling" the educational material of one week of primary or secondary school can be reduced to about 8 to 10 hours a week. The rest of the time, we are taught to be submissive and to fear the authority of the teacher, of the director, of the social worker, of youth protection services, of the police detention centers and of juvenile court.
>
> quoted in Anonymous 2013, 25

In addition to the repressive role, schooling serves a moral regulatory function (what Foucault terms a productive power, producing identity). School involves inculcation into dominant norms, values, and beliefs of the society in which the child lives—state capitalist society. It molds acceptable behaviors within this context (rather than values and behaviors that are expressed against or as an alternative to it). Anarchists argue that as a process of power people need to be disconnected from their experiences and desires to be made ready for undesirable, often unhealthy, work conditions and procedures to which they will be subjected for most of their lives. For the anarchist social movement critic of education under state capitalism:

> A hierarchical society needs school to teach children to be submissive and to renounce their desires, so that children adopt behaviors that support

the established order. School socialization is primary and principle socialization, since it begins at a young age and becomes the main influence on the child, supplanting the family.

Institutionalized socialization is above all a result of the constraints imposed by its agents. Interactions between an individual and their social environment are possible, but they remain under the surveillance and control of the state and corporations since interactions that are not surveilled risk producing a radical social transformation of society.

Anonymous 2013, 26

It is precisely such a radical social transformation that anarchists seek. In doing so, they have developed a range of organizational practices to make their desires a reality. Among the projects that anarchists have undertaken are cooperatives, working groups, alternative unions, collective houses, etc. Perhaps the most recurrent, and among the most valued, of anarchist projects have been free schools (typically located in free spaces or anarchist community centers).

Those seeking realistic positive alternatives to state capitalist social relations desire educational experiences that inform their pursuit of alternatives while bringing those alternatives to life in the here and now of everyday experience (rather that "after the revolution"). As one participant in Toronto's Occupy Free School project suggests: "We desperately need education that is free for the development of the individual personality. This means education that is culturally relevant, and teaches peace and self-determination" (quoted in Kinch 2013, 42). Free schools have been a primary means by which anarchists have sought to make these deeply felt needs real. And they work, if imperfectly.

In addition to sites of knowledge and skill sharing, free schools also provide important opportunities for anarchists and other concerned community members to meet and discuss matters of interest in their lives. It provides a participatory democratic sphere in which people can identify various needs or concerns and speak openly with other about how to resolve problems effectively in concert with their neighbors and/or other residents of the local area. This is a potent resource in a context in which open, participatory democratic opportunities and venues for collaborative problem solving are generally absent for regular folks.

The personally transformative power of anarchist free schools is expressed by many participants. Indeed, I can attest to this from my own experiences over decades (including at several of the venues discussed herein). As rapper and Anarchist Free University alum Illogik (of group Test Their Logik) recounts:

The AFU was amazing vibrant when I first got involved; multiple classes each semester, lot of attendance. The AFU led me to Uprising [bookstore] and then to a now-defunct collective house which all spawned many different activities. It got me plugged into the community and once in, the vehicle that got me there was less important.

quoted in KINCH 2013, 41

Illogik also highlights the role that free schools can play as connectors for broader anarchist and community organizing and shared projects beyond their role as educational spaces. The Anarchist Free Space and Free Skool and its successor the Anarchist Free University in Toronto would provide important inspiration for different projects initiated in other cities outside of Toronto.

Free school participants speak of the sense of conviviality and community that such projects can foster. Free school commentator Niki Thorne, who is a free school alum who went on to write a Master's thesis on free schools, suggests:

FreeSkool, for me, has always been this warm welcoming inspiring space, a community of caring and creative people, and an example of the concrete beautiful projects and initiatives that we can build out of our ideas and ideals. FreeSkool represents creativity and community, and is part of building the kind of world we want to live in.

quoted in KINCH 2013

This speaks to the prefigurative power of these projects. It reflects a key aspect of anarchist projects—the desire to see that means and ends coincide in practice.


2      Building Blocks: Locating Free Schools

Kensington Market is a historically working class neighborhood near downtown Toronto. It had been home to Jewish radicals in the 1930s and 1940s and has maintained its sense of a radical, or at least alternative, haven up to the present. Long a home to anarchists, the Market was the neighborhood in which Emma Goldman spent the last years of her life while in exile from the United States. It is where she died in 1940.

Throughout the 1980s the Market had been home to anarcho-punks who lived and played in the area's several punk venues (from bars to basement parties). The Market punks were important participants in legendary battles against neo-Nazis during that time and through their various efforts drew new genera-tions in the anarcho-punk scene. A number of bands involved in the Kensing-ton scene over the years would go on to achieve widespread acclaim, even in-ternationally. Among these are the bands bunchofuckingoofs and Fucked Up.

Kensington, with its availability of space in historic buildings and its open-ness to bohemian cultures, has provided an important base for anarchist de-velopment. When the Who's Emma? infoshop and DIY punk record shop opened the anarchists had a significant infrastructural space for organizing, awareness raising, and skill development—usually through workshops and meetings. It also had a reliable space for putting on punk shows and mini festivals.

In 1998 the Active Resistance '98 anarchist gathering and conference was organized largely out of Who's Emma? and by people involved with the space. The size and success of the conference served to bring many more people into the movement, in Toronto and beyond. This included people already in To-ronto as well as anarchist inspired activists who moved to Toronto following Active Resistance in order to be involved in the lively movement there. Many, frustrated with the subcultural aspect of Active Resistance, determined to join community based groups involved in anti-poverty work, housing struggles, and anti-racist campaigns.

Within a few years of Active Resistance the Anarchist Free Space and Free Skool, Uprising Books, and the Anarchist Free University had followed in Who's Emma's footsteps, organizing additional spaces in the Market. The Anarchist Free Skool would serve as a crucial entry point for many new anarchists and dozens of people became radicalized through involvement in the space with many becoming experienced organizers who would make substantial contri-butions to political movements in the city over a period of more than a decade (right up to the present). The Free Skool effectively combined relevant real world organizing with theoretical and strategic analysis. It provided a lively pedagogical praxis that inspired and challenged many in local social struggles.

The Anarchist Free University emerged from the ashes of the Free Skool fol-lowing the loss of its physical venue. It would serve as a more traditionally edu-cational project focusing almost exclusively on classes on a range of topics, al-though, of course, participants were also involved in other projects, campaigns, and movements. The AFU shared a house with a radical bike collective (Bike Pirates) sharing labor and resources as well as rent burdens. The AFU would go on to represent one of the longest running projects in Toronto over the last decade. It would contribute to later projects such as Occupy Toronto and the Occupy Freeschool.

Eventually both the Anarchist Free Skool and the Anarchist Free University would become homeless as rising rents in the city made it hard even for relatively stable collectives to maintain venues such as infoshops or punk clubs. The loss of the spaces had real impacts. As Kinch suggests: "Anarchism went a bit further underground. Without a geographical space or a strong activist movement, the AFU stagnated along with the dispersed anarchist scene in general" (2013, 41). At the same time participants in the AFS and AFU would go on to make essential contributions to Occupy Toronto and the Occupy Freeschool as well as free schools and infoshops in other cities.

Both projects served as hubs of skill sharing about free schools and people travelled literally from all over North America to visit and learn how to set up and maintain free schools in their own locales. Projects such as the Free School in Hamilton, Ontario, an industrial city located about an hour southwest of Toronto were directly influenced by the AFS and AFU and invited participants from those projects to join them for initial meetings around setting up their new space. Other projects influenced by the AFS and AFU include the Windsor Workers Action Centre in Windsor, Ontario, and farther afield the Twelfth and Clark anarchist salon in Vancouver which was started by a former AFS participant.

## 3    Out of the Ruins: From G20 Protests to Occupy Free School

The formal dissolution of the AFS and AFU did not mean the end of free school activities in Toronto. Indeed, one aspect of free schools projects is that they instill pedagogical and activist approaches that transcend the spaces of the free schools, percolating through other projects and organizing efforts. Those who experience free school practices come, in various ways, to embody them, expressing them as they engage in their local communities. Such is exemplified in the Toronto context through the emergence of anarchist pedagogical projects, including free schools, in the mass mobilization against the meetings of the G8/G20 global powers in Toronto in 2010 and in Occupy Toronto a year later.

Free school projects developed as important parts of the broad mobilization against the G8/G20 meetings of global capital and national states. The Free School provided crucial venues for raising awareness publicly of concerns with G8/G20 politics and policies and provided a horizontal, participatory, and democratic counterpoint to the elite, exclusive, and anti-democratic closed meetings of the G8/G20. At the same time the Free School helped organizers sharpen their own analyses of capitalism, neoliberalism, and austerity, while providing useful organizing practice beyond the smaller anarchist subcultural context in which free schools often operate.

Popular projects emerged that expanded the scope of free school practice and the range of public interaction. A crew of people came together from one AFU media course to produce a high quality documentary movie, "Tales from the G20," about the mobilization. This provided a useful resource for organizers in Toronto. It also provides a resource for organizers of future such mobilizations and for others seeking information about the G20 and its priorities and policies.

The G8/G20 free school projects took on a life of their own and a Toronto Free School ended up operating for around a year after the G8/G20 meetings left town. Eventually it folded, in part, because organizers had to spend so much time, energy, and resources working on legal defense and popular political-legal education for those arrested and charged during the G8/G20 repression and mass arrests.

Yet the desire for a free school did not dissipate and the experiences of the vitality of the free schools remained strong within participants, providing strong impetus to get started again. When the Occupy wave of protest camps emerged in the fall of 2011, Occupy Toronto benefited from the efforts of various free school participants in the city. As in other cases, the general increase in involvement of younger and/or newer or less experienced political activists in a short period of time, showed a need for educational work to help develop political analysis and share practical skills as well as learn from histories of successful and failed struggles in the city and more broadly. In addition there was a real need for education about issues of oppression, police practices, economic alternatives, and basic survival skills along consensual, communal, and cooperative lines.

A handful of experienced free school organizers including some from the AFS, AFU, and the post-G20 Free School worked to establish the basic infrastructure for the Occupy Free School. Once established, the Occupy Free School was easily maintained by any and all who chose to participate. Anyone could schedule classes simply by listing desired subjects on a whiteboard at the Free School tent and being available at the suggested meeting time.

As might be expected in a case of open struggle, as opposed to day to day living under unequal conditions, classes were typically tied into organizing projects underway at or out of the Occupy camp. This included a class on anarchist theory attended by many involved in community safety at the camp (Kinch 2013). This involvement in the anarchist theory course reflected a real need and desire on the part of participants to develop a theoretical understanding of practical approaches to keeping people safe in a context of active pursuit of freedom, participation, cooperation, and non-hierarchical decision-making. Notably, as in the Anarchist Free Skool, the most popular courses were on anarchist communism and class struggle. Other courses, showing the mix of theory and practice, included ones on gardening and recycled paper arts.

Significantly, and tellingly, the Occupy Free School survived the Occupy camp itself, developing its own life after the camp's collapse. While the loose assembly of Occupy, lacking political coherence and theoretical or practical affinity, fell apart rather spectacularly, the closer, engaged "structure" of the Occupy Free School allowed it to thrive, adapting to radically changed circumstances and providing a common ground for participants to move forward productively in the face of adversity. While the evicted camp dispersed and loose attachments came undone, the Occupy Free School persisted, maintained by people who had learned their theory and practice, strategy and tactics, experientially and collectively together.

The Occupy Free School still meets in a downtown Toronto park each Sunday. It produces a temporarily open and free space, what anarchist theorist Hakim Bey might term a mobile temporary autonomous zone (TAZ) in the heart of the city.


4       Sites of Change: Shifting Priorities, Shifting Practices
        in Free Schools

Free Skools are, almost by definition, heterodox and decentered spaces. Collectives are diverse, changing, and evolving. The viewpoints and priorities of collective members are by no means homogeneous. The Anarchist Free Skool pulsed between two poles that were in creative tension throughout most of the space's existence. On the one hand was an artistic, subcultural, expressive grouping that favored alternative or underground cultural events and dadaesque parties and happenings at the space and classes geared toward cultural dissent (culture jamming, billboard liberation, etc.) and alternative lifestyles. On the other hand was a class struggle grouping that favored community-based local organizing and saw the Free Skool as a resource for organizing. The class struggle grouping participated in anti-poverty movements in the city and was active in anti-gentrification struggles in the specific neighborhood in which the Free Skool was located. The art group argued against fighting the businesses that pushed gentrification in the neighborhood, strangely viewing that struggle as one that did not offer a new cultural vision (despite the cultural underpinnings of much of the gentrification promoters and their expressions against the "poverty cultures" of homeless people). The class struggle group favored classes on theory and practice and historical examples (from urban struggles of the 1970s and 1980s to the anarchist collectives in the Spanish Revolution of the 1930s and in Russia in the revolutionary period).

These two groups managed to coexist and coevolve over a period of five years without interfering too much in each other's work. Eventually more class struggle activists became involved in the space and more activists voluntarily drifted to other, typically gallery, spaces. It should be noted that the growth of alternative globalization movements and struggles after Seattle in 1999, and the influx of young activists inspired by or curious about anarchism into movements, played a part in the growth of the class struggle tendency within the Free Skool. Many of the young activists were looking for real world, practical, means to address issues of economic and social injustice and inequality. While artistic and cultural expressions were personally gratifying they did not meet the desires many had for real structural change and possibilities for socioeconomic resistance.

The issues that mobilized most of the efforts at the Free Skool were those around anti-gentrification, anti-poverty, cop watches and police violence, anti-racist action, and immigration defense and anti-border campaigns. These are all issues that have a connecting thread of class inequality. While these were, and remain, crucial issues, particularly as economic inequality and disparities in wealth grow under regimes of neoliberal austerity, globalization, and deindustrialization (at least in North America), there were noticeable significant gaps in perspective and practice related to Free Skool activities. Issues that were never given enough attention or commitment included feminism, gender diversity, sexual identity, and colonialism.

By the second decade of the twenty-first century these issues have become key components of anarchist organizing, in terms of practice and in terms of perspective (a too long overdue development). This has been driven by the experiences of participants from marginalized groups and identities as they have come up against the ongoing limits of anarchist practice within their own collective efforts and/or as more people from marginalized backgrounds enter anarchist circles and take part in anarchist projects as the movement has grown and expanded. This has also been spurred by the efforts of self-education and personal and political development—learning through everyday practice—of anarchists over time reflecting on the strengths and limitations of their own work and play. While classes on genderfucking, polysexuality, sexual health, or dis/abilities would have been atypical 20 years ago at venues like the Anarchist Free Skool, they have formed significant parts of anarchist work in the 2010s at anarchist spaces like the New Space in Vancouver (unceded Coast Salish territories) where I have been active more recently.

The shifting priorities and concerns within anarchism and anarchist spaces have contributed to an altering of organizational practices and preferences. Spaces like the Free Skool tended to host inclusive events geared toward anarchists of all tendencies as well as non-anarchists who might be interested in learning about anarchism. At current spaces, such as the New Space, events are often particularistic, identity or culture based, driven by and for specific self-identified groups who have too often been excluded or marginalized even within anarchist spaces and movements. In other cases intersections of oppression are identified as bases for solidarity in rethinking anarchist and alternative projects. Thus events like the SB! Festival, organized out of a free space and around anarchist pedagogical projects, are described as:

> An anarcha-feminist, queer, radical, anti-capitalist DIY music festival for anyone who wants it or thinks they might want it. A celebration in smashing patriarchy, showcasing artists who are underrepresented. This festival is for everyone who is disaffected or disgusted by the current independent music culture, dominated by straight, white males.

Spaces developed in the last decades of the twentieth century tended to draw people in and organize on the basis that participants were anarchists first and foremost. Contemporary spaces often involve participation on the basis of personal identity, in which anarchists and non-anarchists organize around a primary identity, say queer, trans, APOC, rather than as anarchists first and foremost. Even where affinity is based on a sense that participants are anarchist, there will more often be altergroupings or caucuses in which participants of particular identifications or backgrounds will self-organize within current spaces. Thus a space may have, in addition to an overall space collective, an APOC caucus, a queer caucus, a women's caucus, a trans caucus, etc., depending on the needs and interests or challenges of participants in specific organizing or social contexts. The caucuses will generally have representation of issues and concerns to the larger collective at broader collective meetings.

In some ways the contemporary anarchist spaces are reminiscent of the awareness and consciousness raising groups of the 1970s and 1980s, geared toward meetings of "affected groups" (discussion circles for women or queers, for example). Such groups and spaces are envisioned as "safe spaces" in which people who self-identify as being of specific groups can meet is a respectful and supportive environment to talk without concern of harassment.

Classes at the Free Skool drew largely on anarchist classics. More contemporary classes tend to draw heavily from other traditions, such as post-colonial theory, critical race theory, whiteness studies, queer theory, etc. Indeed the whole notion of the Free Skool and classes that rather mirror academic courses (course reading list, weekly outline, facilitator, discussion, etc.) has been eclipsed be the issue based singular approach preferred in the current spaces.

In the current spaces there are often single meetings around an issue rather than ongoing classes. This may include a book launch or movie showing in which discussion, often around contributing to an active campaign, occurs rather than the set course format that runs over months.

## 5 Class Issues

Class struggle anarchism, while the most significant trend globally and histori-cally in anarchist movements has always been challenged by more identity based and culture-centric expressions within the movements. This antago-nism has been driven by a number of factors. These include the general antipa-thy to class analysis in North American politics more broadly (including within radical politics). It also reflects the middle strata background of many anar-chist activists and projects in North America (in which an honest critique of class privilege would turn attention to the privilege of some anarchists them-selves) and a lack of understanding of, at least, blue collar working class issues. It also reflects the inroads made by new social movements (NSM) theories and cultural politics within academic milieux from which many anarchist activists have been drawn over the last two decades.

At the same time, and more positively, it reflects the growing cultural (eth-nic, social, sexual, etc.) diversity of participants in anarchist movements in North America. And the growing assertiveness and confidence, individual and collective, of previously marginalized or silenced groups. This includes also in-creased activity around issues of gender, sexuality, identity, and queerness. Other shifts include anarchist responses to ableism. It also reflects the gaps in anarchist sensitivity to and action to address these specific but interlocking forms of domination and inferiorization (Adam 1978).

Contemporary anarchist pedagogies must be attentive to and responsive to the lived experiences, realities, and biases of a diversity of participants and their communities. This means openly questioning and challenging both the composition of anarchist movements (predominantly young white males, for example) and the analytical frameworks of anarchism (the predominance of economism and/or gaps in understanding gender domination, heteronorma-tivity, or colonialism, etc.). To the extent that anarchist collective practices and pedagogical approaches in free schools and other shared projects face these issues honestly and concretely they show significant and necessary growth and development.

At the same time, this does not mean losing or abandoning the important insights of strategic and tactical approaches that do not directly speak to issues of participants' experiences, such as analyses of the wage labor relationship and exploitation under capitalism. So contemporary anarchists must recognize that class (exploitation) matters (as many subculturists overlook or dismiss) while also understanding that the working class has never been monolithic or uniform. It has always been racialized, multiply gendered, sexualized, etc.

More recently a more substantial proportion of anarchists have come to understand the settler colonial character of capitalism on Turtle Island (colonial name North America). Capitalism on Turtle Island did not develop in the same manner as in Europe and European capitalism was in key ways underwritten and bolstered by settler colonialism. At the New Space, an explicit commitment is made to anti-colonial perspectives and to supporting Indigenous groups engaged in struggles.

## 6       Necessary Infrastructures

Like many synthesist anarchist projects, those that bring together anarchists of diverse perspectives and often differing views of strategy and tactics, specific free schools and their projects are often temporary and ephemeral. Economic pressures, like land speculation, commercialization, development, and gentrification, contribute to the collapse of spaces lacking basic means such as the capacity to pay rent. Political pressures, such as arrests of organizers or selective city bylaw enforcement can speed up closures. Evictions by nervous or speculative landlords or police in the case of squatted buildings can shut things down directly. At the same time, anarchist free spaces show the rhizomatic character of many anarchist organizing projects, giving rise to new, but related, manifestations in other areas.

The Toronto free school projects of the last two decades have generally been semi-durable experiments lasting for a few years each in one form before morphing into new projects. There is continuity as some of the people involved in earlier projects carry over their participation to help initiate, develop, and maintain successive projects. At the same time the successive projects show the crucial need for what I term infrastructures of resistance as the life span of the specific school projects is often determined largely (or solely) by the availability of physical space (and associated resources such as books) to host the schools and root them in the broader community (Shantz 2010).

Participants at the various Toronto free school projects are in agreement on the need for physical space in which organizing can occur on a more sustained basis. Kalin Stacey, a participant in the Anarchist Free University reflects on the need for physical space as a key feature of free schools that survive over time. For Stacey:

> One of the things that's really critical for a freeschool is that it's both a decentralized and learning project, but also a community building project. The best scenario for an established freeschool that sticks around is to have a radical community centre/social space, autonomous space that also is sustainable and can provide a meeting place. That's something the anarchist free school that happened in the late '90s [and early 2000s] in Kensington had that made it really effective. And, when they lost the space, they lost the school.
>
> quoted in KINCH 2013, 41

This speaks to the pressing need, felt by participants, for infrastructures of resistance in anarchist organizing projects. It also speaks to the need, also understood by participants, to bring community struggles together with educational efforts. This is the key part played by infrastructures of resistance. Not only do they provide reliable resources necessary for ongoing organizing work (meeting space, phone lines, food preparation, etc.). They also provide venues in which people involved in diverse and seemingly disparate struggles can come into contact with one another, see commonalities and seek common ground, and strategize around the best ways to act in solidarity to develop their struggles mutually. Such infrastructures of resistance allow for a certain "collaborative advantage" such that limited resources in labor or materials might have a greater impact when deployed in conjunction with united (if not unified) struggles through shared projects and/or perspectives.

The experiences of the Toronto free schools would seem to confirm Paolo Friere's argument that for liberation education to be successful, and contribute to meaningful social change, it must be linked to a broader project of human life more generally.

Free schools have played important parts in the development of anarchist movements in urban centers like Toronto and Vancouver from the middle 1990s to the present. At the same time those schools have thrived mostly when involved in broader community organizing efforts, when they have had direct and vital intersections with political organizing and mobilization in the neighborhoods in which the schools are situated.

The challenges faced by free schools, in starting up, sustaining themselves, and in rising from the ruins are those faced by movements themselves. Infrastructures of resistance are necessary to provide more durable bases for movements to continue and develop and to prevent the dissipation of efforts as struggles ebb and wane. As Kinch reflects:

> Organically connected with the anti-authoritarian organizing scenes in the city, liberation education has risen and fallen with the tide of militancy in the city. Wresting physical and organization space from capitalism for the projects we need is a difficult task, but it's one that has to be done as we move forward.
> We can't always fight the system head on. We also have to build the systems that sustain ourselves and our struggles as we move out of the margins to really challenge the capitalism and the state.
>
> KINCH 2013, 42

And to build alternatives in the here and now of everyday life. Infrastructures of resistance provide the necessary sustenance of struggles. They are the foundations of the new world in the shell of the old.

Such projects are highly labor intensive and require a great deal of day to day maintenance to keep them running effectively. This reality often runs up against ant-work attitudes and the preferences for play and "hanging out" that are perhaps too prevalent in anarchist subcultural scenes. While many anarchists express a healthy rejection and criticism of imposed capitalist work and work discipline they often fail to distinguish between self-valorizing sustenance work (required to keep people and communities thriving) and the capital valorizing tasks associated with the job form (and the sale of labor power to an owner of property).

## 7     Conclusion: Context Matters

For anarchists free schools are crucial resources within broader processes of contesting the domestication of dissent and building authentic forms of rebellion and resistance. They offer means by which people can keep the animal from being kicked out of us to return to Halley's notion noted earlier. As one anarchist critics argues:

> The industrial system has found in the education model a rational way to domesticate the exploited, thus allowing for easier recuperation of resistance by redirecting it into institutional channels, like union negotiation

or political reformism. The rebels who have interiorized the values trans-
mitted by school try to retouch the repressive machine, rather than destroy it, and a domesticated child is one who only expresses themselves
in the moment that the teacher (the state) allows them.

Authentic rebellion starts in the streets and then builds alternatives both
to corporatized universities and to the dominant society.

Anonymous 2013, 27

The post-Seattle/post-9/11 period has seen anarchism grow dramatically in
terms of influence (both in the streets and in the academy) and in terms of legitimacy (many now at least have some sense of what anarchism is as compared with twenty years ago). In addition, anarchism has developed as perhaps
the most significant idea system or perspective within radical social movements in North America, supplanting Marxism and its various Leninist and
Maoist variants.

Free schools, as incubators of anarchist thought and action, are both products of and producers of their specific social contexts, local concerns and issues. They are representative of the struggles that animate (and are animated
by) them. Thus, in Toronto, where issues of housing, homelessness, and cuts to
social welfare for poor people, along with deindustrialization and unemployment—and policies designed to criminalize poor and homeless people—were
pressing political concerns, the AFS oriented itself toward defense of homeless
people in a neighborhood facing, indeed undergoing, gentrification. Many anarchists at the Free Skool had experienced poverty and homelessness first
hand. In Vancouver, where issues of resource extraction and extreme energy
and pipelines are major areas of intense local struggles, and environmental
politics are often entry points for politicization and/or radicalization, members have devoted time and resources to defend the land and to support Indigenous communities facing the perils of extractive industries and capitalist
land development.

CHAPTER 5

# Class Conflicts: Anarchists and Workplace Organizing

Perhaps ironically, one of the areas of organizing in which contemporary anarchists in the Canadian and US state contexts have been greatly lacking has been around workplace and worker organizing. I say ironically because anarchism emerged as part of the international workers movement against capitalism and exploitation and was, for a long period, among the leading forces within that movement, including within the First International. And the concerns of anarchist activists and theorists alike were very much driven by the pressing need to overcome capitalist exploitation and property relations, with particular attention to the productive power of the working classes and their capacity to withdraw and redirect labor. By the first decades of the twentieth century, however, anarchism has been severely detached from the working class more broadly and from the majority of workplace organizing efforts more specifically. As many commentators have pointed out most self-identified anarchists and the projects they are involved in are decidedly of "middle class" (white collar or professional) backgrounds and/or déclassé in character (that is they are social class dropouts, who have left their familial class location at least temporarily or culturally, or do not hold to any class identity).

At the same time there are very real social reasons for the historic separation of anarchists and workers movements in the US and Canada. On the one hand there are the extensive histories of substantial repression directed at anarchist workers and working class organizations. Among the significant state actions were the waves of violence and criminalization directed against anarchist following the Haymarket battles and the bombing of 1886. This included the mass arrests of anarchist union organizers and the execution of anarchist workers for political reasons (in the absence of evidence linking them to the Haymarket attack). The post-Haymarket targeting of anarchist workers really ushered in a period of state directed assaults on anarchists and of repression particularly against migrant communities who were associated in nativist discourses with anarchist sympathies (including Italians and Germans notably). By the 1910s these torrents of state repression were given infamous formal expression in the Palmer Raids initiated by US Attorney General A. Mitchell Palmer. Under the Palmer Raids, between 1919 and 1920, as many as 6000 people were arrested with many of those arrested being deported. The Palmer

Raids were preceded by an extended period of repression from February 1917 to November 1919, during which federal agents deported sixty so-called "aliens" from among some 600 arrested for anarchist associations. Additional raids culminated in the mass deportation of 249 people on December 21 aboard a single so-called "Red Ark," the Buford. Among those deported was "the world's most dangerous woman" Emma Goldman.

Similar repressive measures were enacted against anarchists in the Canadian state context over this same period. In 1919 the Winnipeg General Strike, in which workers mobilized for an eight hour day, the demand of Haymarket faced the unified response of the Canadian government and corporations. On a solidarity march of workers and veterans of World War One who allied themselves with their fellow workers was attacked by the forces of the Royal North-West Mounted Police (precursors to the Royal Canadian Mounted Police or RCMP) with two workers being murdered by police and 34 others injured. In response to the strike foreign born workers were targeted and the Immigration Act revised to allow the Canadian government more easily to deport people.

The cumulative effect of these sustained assaults on anarchist organizers, organizations, and communities was devastating. In some ways it can be said that anarchist movements and politics never recovered from the decades of repression through the first decades of the twentieth century. By the end of the Second World War anarchism was merely a remnant of its former presence in the US and Canada.

The other factor in the decline of anarchism from the 1920s was the simultaneous rise of Leninist Marxism following the triumph of the Bolsheviks in Russia. The ascendance of the Bolsheviks and apparent model for revolutionary success provided in the shape of Leninism meant that the vanguard party would become the organizational form guiding would be revolutionaries and revolutionary movements internationally. The defeat of the anarchists and anarcho-syndicalists in Spain during the Spanish Revolution by the combined forces of fascism/Nazism, with an assist from the undermining efforts of the Stalinist machinery, would prove a knockout blow for anarchism that would see the movement, as an element of working class resistance, driven to the margins or underground for decades.

The outcome of state and capitalist efforts to stamp anarchist organizing out of working class movements and cultures has been that the current generations of anarchist organizers have lacked direct access to or contact with meaningful anarchist presence within the working class and within workplaces. It also means that anarchism, rather than being readily recognized as part of the history and heritage of working class movements and communities, is misunderstood, ignored, or unseen by contemporary workers. Thus, there is virtually no industry where a living memory of anarchism as part of working class organizing is a familiar or present part of contemporary experiences of workers in that industry. This is distinct from histories of socialism and even communism which are recognizable as part of the histories or workers' efforts in, for example, auto.

The attacks on anarchism have also been an attack on collective working class memory and on working class infrastructures of resistance. Among the too often overlooked losses have been horizontal, egalitarian, and participatory, radically democratic, forms of workers' organizing as well as direct action approaches to workplace mobilization and contestation with ownership and management. This has coincided with, provided another side of, the entrenchment of hierarchical, top-down business union models within labor movements. Anarcho-syndicalist forms of organizing, and the histories of syndicalist organizing within working class struggles have been obscured within the movements and beyond.

1        The Classless Class?

Another factor in the separation of anarchists from workplace organizing relates to the class composition of recent anarchist movements themselves. There is an ideological and structural component to the class character of many anarchist projects in the Canadian and US state contexts.

Anarchism became something of an activist subcultural tendency. That is, rather than emerging somewhat organically from the needs of specific oppressed or exploited communities in struggle, as it had historically among the working classes and poor, anarchism by the late twentieth century had become something of an activist identity or milieu for people from diverse backgrounds who had developed an oppositional stance to any of multiple aspects of social injustice. Typically it became an ideological position adopted by people who had become radicalized as activists (often detached from their communities or backgrounds).

To large degrees these activists were from middle strata (white collar or professional) backgrounds and/or were students, rather than, for example blue collar workers or people who viewed themselves primarily as working class. This class composition and its déclassé identities actually had an ideological underpinning. This ideological buttressing was located in strands of post-New Left theorizing which found particularly fertile ground within emerging anarchist perspectives.

This should not be taken to say that these are the only aspects of anarchist orientations to class and class struggle. Indeed during the missing link period of anarchist movements, from the post-New Left period of the 1980s up to the early alternative globalization movements of 1999 Seattle, many anarchists involved themselves in a variety of class struggle and workplace oriented organizations (typically federations or groupings). Some of these included the Industrial Workers of the World (the historic syndicalist union), the Workers' Solidarity Movement (WSM), and the Love and Rage Federation among other smaller local groupings and projects. The point of this chapter, though, is not to explore the maintenance of class struggle perspectives and projects in the 1980s and 1990s but, rather, to explore contemporary workplace oriented projects and organizing.

## 2      A Special Strategic Character

For class struggle anarchists and anarchists involved in workplace organizing and mobilization the importance of class and workers' control is not a matter of identity. Rather it is an issue of strategy, tactics, and an analysis of the power of the exploited to confront and challenge the concentration of power and inequality in state capitalist society in a manner that might actually disrupt existing power relations and bring powerholders to crisis. For class struggle anarchists, as indeed for revolutionary Marxists, organized, active, workers in their workplaces have a particular, special, capacity to interfere with and break processes and relations of exploitation in a way that can potentially end those relations and processes. The power of the strike or workplace occupation, for example, does, in fact, end, or at least suspend, practices and relations of exploitation in that particular moment, with potential to disrupt those relations and processes more broadly as workplace actions spread (in solidarity or on their own basis). Strikes are potent examples because they show unambiguously who really produces social value in society and at the same time it expresses, straightforwardly, who holds productive power within workplaces. This is a power that is unique to workers mobilized in workplaces and it has effects that cannot be approached by social actions like the occupy camps, protests, or demonstrations which largely leave relations of production of value and exploitation unmolested, even unthreatened.

Workplace actions have a different character in other regards as well. For one thing they are not based on moral or ideological appeals. Rather they are typically expressions of the direct needs (short and long term) of the people

involved. These can include material needs such as health, wellbeing, time for
family and community, sustenance, etc. as well as immaterial, or ideational
ones such as life satisfaction, enjoyment, etc. Even more they often encompass
or speak to related needs (for a clean community, preservation of nature, future for one's children, etc.). In addition they are expressions, not of moral appeal or persuasion (though they can include these) but of social relations (the
real labor in value production that is being exploited by capital/owners/bosses,
for example). They perform a pedagogical role as well in teaching the exploited
and oppressed that they have real social power, collectively, and in deploying
it, collectively, they can win. And it provides some examples how to do so. This
is, then, foundationally distinct from other forms of collective action, such as
protests, demonstrations, and occupy camps, which rely on, depend upon,
moral appeals to authorities and which leave people in dependent positions
vis-à-vis authorities.

This stands in contrast with the more hierarchical, authoritarian, often undemocratic, forms of the formal union bureaucracies. For most anarchists,
unions have lost any emancipatory capacities they might have once held. Indeed, for many anarchists, unions were never geared toward emancipation
from capitalism, apart from the examples posed by a few syndicalist unions
such as the Industrial Workers of the World in North America or the Conféder-
ation National de Trabajo (CNT).

## 3    Anarchist Perspectives on Unionism: Labor Organizing and Rank-and-File Resistance

From an anarchist perspective, unions manage the labor and wage relationship. They do not oppose it. They represent a bureaucratic structure outside of
the workplace rather than a democratic free association of workers within it.
In fact, mainstream unions often work to stamp out or disband such associations where they do emerge in workplaces and challenge management and
ownership. Unions were readily co-opted and indeed co-opted themselves to
become little more than mid-level managers of the contract and a range of
working conditions (around pay, hours, job descriptions, vacations). Unions
became disciplinary agencies against the autonomous activities of the membership. They prevent or manage strikes, job actions, sabotage, and occupations. They mobilize against absenteeism.

Union officials represent a new, privileged social strata, neither workers nor
employers (though often they do employ office staff who are sometimes forced
to strike against them). Nowadays they are not even taken from the ranks of
the working class, or the workforce they actually represent, but rather from

professional strata and students. They develop economic interests that are different from, even opposed to, rank-and-file workers. Their concern is not primarily with real improvements for the membership but rather increased salaries, benefits, conditions, and status for themselves. Typically they are happy to maintain an established level of privilege rather than do something out of the ordinary to gain potential increases for the membership (or risk losses for themselves).

Typically, union officials seek bargain with (rather than challenge) management to get only enough for members to keep them from being restless. Usually in negotiations they work to convince members that this limited result was all that was available and the members should, thus, accept it despite their disappointment. They do not prioritize what workers actually need and desire. Often they do not even consult or share information with members.

Bosses and governments would rather deal with people who have the economic interests of labor brokers than with the laborers themselves, who are often hostile to bosses and government representatives alike. Unions have become deeply integrated into the system of exploitation as institutions of capital and investment. This occurs most notably in the growth of union pension funds which have billions in holdings in capitalist enterprises. The success of the funds depends on profitability—exploitation—and impels support for capitalist markets.

In some ways the role of radical capacity of unions is a moot point since unionization rates have declined to miniscule proportions in industries in the United States and Canada. There is presently an eight percent unionization rate in non-governmental workplaces in the United States. It is likely that the union movement will not recover, at least in its previously understood and recognized forms. As Herod suggests:

> Even if current labor activists succeed and rebuild unions to what they once were, can we expect these newly refashioned unions to accomplish more than previous ones did, at the height of the unionization drives of a strong labor movement—a movement that was embedded in communist, socialist, and anarchist working-class cultures that have now been obliterated? Hardly. (2007, 29)

So the door is wide open, the floor cleared for new forms of working class workplace association or organization. Yet, there have been only halting, experimental attempts to fill the void. Some have been false starts while others hold some promise. Those that are most promising suggest a coming together of rank-and-file activists and militants.

For anarchists and radical rank-and-file workers, labor organizing, and unions, should not be geared toward immediate economic gains limited to the workers of a single workplace or trade but should seek to disrupt and end the existing industrial framework. It should have as a goal the abolition of the existing division of labor and the wages system.

Anarchism seeks the social condition in which one is free to choose the mode and condition of work, where one experiences the freedom to work and work in freedom (Goldman 1969). Its goal is achieving "the freest possible expression of the latent powers of the individual" (Goldman 1969, 55). This is the expression of what Oscar Wilde calls "a perfect personality," one who is not threatened or rendered precarious. As Goldman describes it:

> One to whom the making of a table, the building of a house, or the tilling of the soil, is what the painting is to the artist and the discovery to the scientist,—the result of inspiration, of intense longing, and deep interest in work as a creative force. That being the ideal of Anarchism, its economic arrangements must consist of voluntary productive and distributive associations, gradually developing into free communism, as the best means of producing with the least waste of human energy. Anarchism, however, also recognizes the right of the individual, or numbers of individuals, to arrange at all times for other forms of work, in harmony with their tastes and desires. (1969, 55–56)

There can be no meaningful workplace strike without some workplace organizing. Militant organizing in the workplace requires rank-and-file alternatives, such as flying squads, working groups, and direct action groups.

## 4    Rank-and-File Organizing: Anarchic Forms

Rank-and-file forms of Informal organizations, from informal work groups to committees to flying squads already take organizational approaches, forms and practices, that are anarchic in nature and align with the types of organizational approach that anarchists have long argued for and pursued. Thus, there is a real affinity between common rank-and-file organizational approaches and anarchist organizing.

This should not be overlooked or underestimated. Too often in contemporary discussions of movement forms, pursuing an interest in new forms of horizontalist, decentralized, egalitarian organization, focus is directed to community movement practices like the Occupy camps and popular assemblies, or certain grassroots social movement groups. Yet informal workplace groupings and rank-and-file organizational practices are rarely raised or given any attention (let alone sustained discussions). This is unfortunate on two fronts. One, it overlooks significant organizational practices that provide important models of horizontalist, decentralized, egalitarian organizing within hierarchical, undemocratic social environments (as most workplaces are). Secondly, overlooking rank-and-file organizing reinforces a dual notion that the impetus for horizontalist, egalitarian organizational innovations comes from outside of the working class in their workplace settings, from people as worker, and that those looking to learn from such organizational efforts should look elsewhere while simultaneously reinforcing notions that workers' organizing inevitably occurs through bureaucratic and hierarchical structures.

## 5    Flying Squads

A flying squad is simply a rapid response team of workers who are ready and committed to spring into action, for whatever reasons they deem necessary and appropriate, on relatively short notice. It consists of a group of workers who commit to make themselves available for actions and to contact one another when mobilization is necessary. Typically they mobilize for workplace related actions such as picket support, work refusals, support for workers dealing with management and so on. This can include solidarity work and support for workers in their own workplace or, often, for workers in other workplaces. This can include strike support but also direct actions to support ununionized workers facing, for example, job loss, harassment, withholding of pay, etc.

Notably, flying squads are also deployed for purposes of community defense. That is they mobilize for actions that are not immediately workplace issues. Examples include immigration defense to halt deportations, tenant defense to stop evictions, and support for unemployed people making social assistance claims. In this way, as anarchist participant point out, the flying squads extend beyond a limited trade union consciousness to express a certain class consciousness to contest broader social attacks that have negative impacts on the working class (as migrants, as tenants, as precarious workers, as unemployed, etc.). They work to bring working class resources from specific unions, for example, to the class more broadly especially within local communities in which flying squad members work and live.

Flying squads have a straightforwardly (and one might suggest radically) horizontal, egalitarian, and participatory democratic structure. Indeed it is such a truly minimalist form of organization that calling it a structure might

seem a bit too grandiose. In fact flying squads need consist of little more, orga-
nizationally or structurally, than a group of people who share a contact list that
allows anyone in the flying squad to contact anyone else. Typically contact information includes phone numbers and verbal communication is preferred to,
say, email communication. Often, depending on the size of the flying squad,
there will be designated callers who will commit to taking responsibility to call
specified people on the list to let them know of a mobilization. With the contact list any member can initiate the flying squad to action by contacting callers to let other members know that the flying squad needs to be at a particular
location at a particular time for a particular reason or action. So the person
initiating a mobilization may only need to call the callers who will contact
their designated members. As everyone has the full list of members designated
callers can be rotated and none holds any power within the flying squad.

In fact the flying squad structure makes it a readily available organizing option for any grouping of people. A handful of people willing, and committed, to
ac, and willing to share their contact details with one another can form a flying
squad.

Flying squads are structured and operate along the lines of what anarchists
refer to as affinity groups. They bring together people on an equal basis to carry
out specific tasks or accomplish specific goals. Relations are voluntary and
based on trust and communication rather than on command and control. Participants have expressed commitments to one another.

Flying squads typically eschew formal meeting structures. They are not
about the cycle of meetings that overtake much activist energies (and patience). Usually meetings and discussions occur during or immediately before
or after the flying squad action. Yet the flying squad has the flexibility to come
together quickly to discuss emerging issues or to prepare to act to head off an
impending crisis situation.

This is not to say that flying squads forego strategizing or developing tactical
analyses of shifting social issues and considering their most effective interventions in social struggles. Political analyses develop directly through actions and
reflection on those actions. Flying squads, because they are action oriented,
provide excellent venues for regularly engaging strategic and tactical issues
and for reconsidering and revising approaches, if you will pardon, on the fly.

Anarchist involvement in flying squads within their own mainstream union
contexts has largely provided means for direct participation with fellow workers within their own unions, workplaces, and communities. It provides an opportunity to bring in horizontalist, egalitarian, and direct action approaches at
the same time as building solidarity with co-workers and community members. It also helps to build a fighting rank-and-file perspective, orientation, and

capacity within specific unions and workplaces. It certainly also allows a space to discuss explicitly anarchist ideas, strategies, tactics, and histories with fellow workers who might otherwise have little or no access to such knowledge.

Because anarchist workers are not typically concentrated within specific workplaces involvement is usually on an individual basis, or in twos or threes within a particular union flying squad that will include varying numbers of workers of diverse political backgrounds (and, of course, those who subscribe to no particular political perspective).

Some anarchists have worked to build broader cross-union flying squads that bring together more numerous groupings of anarchists across a locale into one flying squad.

Anarchists associated with the anarchist communist collective Punching Out initiated an autonomous flying squad to engage in ongoing, regular support for striking workers in and around Toronto. The autonomous flying squad was organized along horizontal, egalitarian lines, on an anarchist model, with no formal leadership structure or formal connection to official union leadership structures. That is, it maintained autonomy from formal union structures even as some of its participants were themselves members of mainstream unions.

The autonomous flying squad was particularly active in supporting workers in small union locals (and small workplaces) during strikes that were otherwise given little support from mainstream union channels, such as official unions and local and labor councils. Notably the workers in the striking locals were often of migrant background and not English first language speakers. This had further served to isolate some of the workers from more established union channels. In addition in the case of workers in small workplaces their struggles were not viewed as high priority for official union structures, even in their own broader union federations (because they were viewed as high cost and high maintenance relative to dues income).

The autonomous flying squad provided a venue in which anarchists could meet and strategize as well as a vehicle for putting their ideas into action. It was geared both toward advancing class solidarity, and showing solidarity in action, as well as offering a pole of attraction for anarchist activists who are interested in and committed to class struggle organizing. By taking part in workplace related and strike actions in particular, the autonomous flying squad successfully brought anarchist ideas and organizing practices directly to working people in the context of contributing to actual struggles in which the workers were engaged and which were meaningful to them. Thus, the autonomous flying squad could effectively overcome some of the "strangeness" or "otherness" of anarchism for rank-and-file workers who might never have encountered anarchy in anything beyond caricatured corporate media or state accounts. At the same time, the autonomous flying squad simultaneously provided a way to take anarchists out of the subcultural spaces or "activist ghettos" to which much anarchist activity has been relegated.

An autonomous flying squad can also provide a useful organizing resource for anarchists who are looking to organize their own unorganized workplace. It offers a venue for members to invite fellow workers in their own workplace to participate in the absence of a union or collectively organized workplace. In some cases it can provide a space for organizing worker-members' workplaces or as a form of collective support before or on the way to organizing a workplace. It gives invited workers an opportunity to experience some of the support that organizing can offer for their own situations as well as partial protection against their employer.

Flying squads also serve as nodal points connecting rank-and-file activists of different workplaces and/or unions. And they do so through solidarity in action. They allow for an interconnection of struggles at a base, grassroots, level, that is distinct from the top down, and often symbolic approaches, of more bureaucratically structured formal union organizations. They can serve as a conduit for broader rank-and-file organizing and direct actions. Too often interactions between unionists across workplaces and unions occur only at the level of formal representatives in federations or labor councils. Flying squads directly link rank-and-file workers, connecting them in face-to-face activities.

## 6      Working Groups

Anarchist workplace organizers have also worked to build broader class-wide infrastructures within existing union structures. One example includes the CUPE 3903 Anti-Poverty Working Group (APWG) (a post-secondary workers local of the Canadian Union of Public Employees). The Working Group acts beyond the expectations of traditional unionism to assist people (members and non-members) experiencing problems with collection agencies, landlords, bosses, and police and to help anyone having difficulties with welfare or other government bureaucracies. The APWG is available to assist students and non-students studying or living in Northwest Toronto. As they put it in one of their leaflets distributed publicly:

> Been laid off without back pay? Landlord keep your rent deposit or threaten you with huge rent increases? Building lacking proper repairs? Being hassled by security guards? Collection agents harassing you or your

family? Need help getting disability assistance? If you've been dealing with any of these or similar situations then the Anti-Poverty Working Group may be able to help you out. Assistance can be offered for anything from filling out government forms properly to taking direct action against an employer or landlord who is ripping you off. You decide the best approach to deal with your situation and the APWG helps with resources and people to get it done. Recognizing that "established channels" rarely work in favour of poor people the working group is committed to taking whatever action is necessary to get people what they need.

Anarchists also played a part in the formation of the Indigenous Solidarity working group within CUPE 3903, though it must be said that the main impetus was given by libertarian socialists. The Indigenous Solidarity working group was initiated out of solidarity efforts involving Indigenous and non-Indigenous activists involved in solidarity work for the Six Nations land reclamation at Caledonia, Ontario.

## 7      Conclusion

Flying squads are set apart from more traditional formal union structures in a few ways. One is that they engage primarily in direct action and immediate confrontation with authorities (whether managers, bosses, state officials, etc.). The other is that they are not predominantly limited to specific workplace issues. Flying squads do mobilize to address issues that arise in the workplaces of the flying squad members, from harassment by managers, to health and safety issues, to working conditions in general, and more, to be sure. But they go beyond the bounds of workplace issues to address issues of community concern more broadly. In this way they express class solidarity on a broader footing, recognizing that the working class includes the unemployed, the poor, the homeless, migrants, stay at home caregivers, students, etc. They also express a perspective that collective working class resources, as in unions, are class resources rather than the private property of specific unions, for example.

Even more the flying squads and working groups express working class action beyond the limitations of legally recognized and limited activities such as those in which mainstream unions are typically employed, typically around management of the collective agreement. The commitment to direct action, solidarity pickets, actions against government offices and officials, etc. takes flying squads and working groups beyond the legally circumscribe activities of mainstream unions and may even place them outside of the law.

While not strictly or formally anarchist projects all of these examples of rank-and-file organizing have been anarchic in structure and practice. And all of the specific examples provided here have had anarchists involved in them directly as participants.

# CHAPTER 6

# Cyber Disobedience: Organizing Anarchy Online

Anarchists have pursued visions of political autonomy, sovereignty, and community in online practice. They have challenged state and corporate governance structures and sought alternative governance structures and social relations (based on openness and self-determination). Very early on anarchist perspectives became key frameworks for online actors and provided crucial guidance for development of cyberspace for many, both those who participated in and those who imaged the internet. Indeed, it could be said, though it has been under-examined and under-theorized, that the development of the internet and the place of anarchist ideas within early debates and discussions of the internet, and its various webs, played a large part in the revitalization of anarchist ideas in the last decade of the twentieth century, even before (or alongside really) the alternative globalization movements ahead of the breakthrough into broader public consciousness following the Seattle eruption in 1999.

Online activists found through the internet the promise and possibility for spaces of inter/action to thrive beyond the realm of traditional powers, particularly nation states. Of course, the internet has proven to be a realm of struggle, like any other in state capitalist contexts, and states have moved quickly to enclose the online (imagined) commons through various mechanisms of surveillance, control, and repression. This has led some commentators to speak of struggles over cyberspace as new enclosures, harkening to the struggles over the natural commons that marked (initiated) the spark of capitalist development. Despite the early hopes, anarchism was never a sure, or even a likely, thing in cyberspace.

## 1    Anarchy in Cyberspace

Early crypto anarchy theorist Peter Ludlow suggests that anarchism became such a central issue of interest in cyberspace in part because the widespread availability of certain technologies renders certain anarchist ideas not only possible but perhaps inevitable. As he argues: "That is, cryptography and related technologies like anonymous remailers and electronic cash may undermine the concentrations of power that we are currently familiar with (nation states, for example), thus allowing us to take on substantially more individual responsibility" (2001, xvii). And this relates to the emergence of new, possibly utopian, governance structures. Ludlow suggests: "And perhaps the Internet provides the opportunity for utopias to emerge in various remote corners of cyberspace—in various 'islands in the Net,' to borrow a phrase from Bruce Sterling" (2001, xvii). The public internet developed, and develops, through a convergence of accessible technologies and media and anarchic self-directed practices. And these build up (and build through) their own self-governance practices.

Yet the self-governing governance practices of the internet are perhaps more ambiguous than is generally recognized or remarked upon. While some certainly create opportunities and possibilities for opposition to state and corporate modes of regulation and control others play into and reinforce neoliberal forms of governance and obedience. The refusal of corporate and state interchange, and exploitation, is accompanied by new forms of exploitation and spreading commercialization, and the development of commercial subjectivities among internet "users."

New technologies and resources allow for possibilities to carve out space for activities that are beyond the control of nation states and corporations. The internet facilitates the spread and connectivity of virtual communities, which in some sense anarchism has always been. That is, there is no anarchist homeland or hereditary anarchism. Anarchism, like other voluntary groupings consists of intentional networks. The internet has grown through the spread of virtual communities and reinforces the types of arrangements anarchism, as for other subaltern or subterranean groupings, has always comprised.

From the early days of the internet commentators have espoused the affinity between the Net and anarchism (see Barbrook, Hirsh). These commentators and many practitioners saw the Net as a form of actual anarchy in action due especially to the apparent absence of an external, imposed authority and the self-direction, autonomy, and liberty expressed in Net practices.

Even as the authorities have made their impositions felt more really and forcefully, for many the real, true form of the internet remains anarchy. And many are willing to fight for the Net as a space of anarchy and to oppose the authoritarian interlopers.

## 2     Online Activist Organizations

Early intersections and networks of hacker activists converged around the Chaos Computer Club (CCC). The Chaos Computer Club was founded early on in the digital age, in 1981, and stands not only as one of the most durable but also one of the most influential community organizations addressing especially the security and privacy aspects of contemporary technologies particularly in the German-speaking world. CCC is Europe's largest association of hackers and is organized in a decentralized manner. There are estimated to be about 5,500 hacker members of the Chaos Computer Club. The CCC is organized in 25 so-called "Erfakreisen" (regional hackerspaces) and in many more smaller groupings, the "Chaostreffs." The many physical hackerspaces in and around Germany share a common bond with the CCC through commitment to their stated hacker ethics.

CCC has been active in developing and disseminating analyses of a range of both technical and social issues. Their overarching focus has been on surveillance, privacy, freedom of information, hacktivism, and data security. Toward this end they produce occasional publications on specific themes and issues. In terms of activism the CCC organizes real world campaigns and special events, as well a active lobbying. Their technical work involves anonymizing services and communication infrastructure.

Their hacker congress, an original one still held on an old school face to face conference basis is quite large and well attended. The CCC has hosted this annual Chaos Communication Congress since 1984 and still edits its publication *Die Datenschleuder*.

Many of the women hackers who participated in the CyberFeminist International (meetings held in Rotterdam) were from the CCC. The CyberFeminist International targeted both patriarchal structures of oppression and exploitation of labor within the cyber industries and cybernetic capitalism and the marginalization of women within hacking movements and cultures. Women in the CyberFeminist International focused very much on issues of production and reproduction within hacking spaces and prioritized the organization of work (recognizing unequal distributions of labor within hacking and alternative media spaces).

The oldest autonomous service provider in Europe is the ECN (European Counter Network—ecn.org). The ECN provides free email accounts, mailing lists, and websites to organizations, activists, and movements that are explicitly involved in a range of social struggles, including around issues of human rights, freedom of speech, and information freedom in Italy and elsewhere. Years before sites such as YouTube and Vimeo were created, ECN pioneered a platform called NGV at which people could upload and share video of relevance to social justice struggles. Notably, especially in a context of growing far Right movements in Europe and beyond, the ECN has espoused an explicitly anti-fascist politics. In the twenty-first century in fact the ECN has prioritized work with anti-fascist and anti-Nazi movements across Europe. Beyond technical services and support, the ECN provides physical space and material resources to political and social organizing centers.

Perhaps the most influential online activist group in the North American context is TAO Communications formed in Toronto, Ontario in 1998. Taking its name as a play on words (The Amazing Orangutans, Tasty Appetizing Oranges) TAO was from the start an explicitly anarchist grouping which saw its work as building real world organizing spaces as well as providing online resources and skills. TAO was explicitly syndicalist in its orientation, understanding its members as tech workers in a tech economy that they sought to confront, and abolish. TAO eventually formed a job shop of the Industrial Workers of the World as an expression of their commitment to workers control. TAO provided labor as a gift to militant anti-poverty organizations like the Ontario Coalition Against Poverty and TAO members were instrumental in the formation of anti-borders and migrant defense movements in Canada. A TAO worker brought the banner 'No One Is Illegal' to North American organizing after attending a hacktivist conference in Amsterdam. TAO served as an incubator and seed bed for other radical online groupings, many which have gone on to outlive the originals.

TAO also showed the circulation of inspiration and influence across movements and historical time in that they drew explicitly on the organizing practices and principles of the Black Panther Party, an organization very much rooted in day to day real world struggles of the exploited and oppressed. TAO's public statement of identity, its basis of unity, gives a sense of their approach and orientation to organizing. It reads in part:

> We organize in order to defend and expand public space and the right to self-determination. We create knowledge through independent public interest research, and distribute it freely through participatory education. We actively promote the establishment of worker-owned and operated autonomous zones. Under the belief that information should be free, we operate against capital or market-regulated forms of political, economic and cultural organization, and towards socially just, ecologically sound, international liberation. We advocate democratic exercise of the means of production to help achieve these beliefs. We also create tactical arts intended for such practical and inspirational application, as to encourage other autonomous groups and individuals to join us in our struggle for democracy. What follows are the agreed upon demands and beliefs of our federation, although not exclusively, or by any limitations:

(1) We want freedom. We want the power to resist tyranny and inevitability. We believe in community based participatory democracy arising from direct action and public accountability. In this we believe that people will not be free until we are all able to effectively engage our society as equals in a process of voluntary co-operation. This process includes the freedom for everyone to become, belong, and just plain be, in a manner that does not violate the rights of others.

(2) We want full employment and support for all people, engendering political, economic, and social egalitarianism. We believe that every person is inherently entitled to either full employment or a guaranteed income. We believe that the means of production should be placed in the hands of the people, so that communities are able to organize full employment, providing a responsible standard of living which sustainably tries to meet the needs of all people now and in the future.

(3) We want an end to the robbery of our communities by capitalists. We believe that that the global ruling class and its corporate economic entities have been built on plunder, pillage, conquest, and tyranny. We demand an end to economic slavery and dependence, with the cancellation of all debt, and restitution to be paid to all aboriginal and formerly colonized peoples.

(4) We want free and decent housing, fit for the shelter of human beings. We believe that if the landowners and landlords will not freely give decent housing, then the land should be made into co-operatives, so that local communities, if necessary with aid, can build and take decent housing fit for their people.

(5) We want free participatory education for all people that allows us to explore the diverse histories found in our cultures, and the diverse roles we all play in the present-day society. We believe in an education system that enables people to develop a knowledge of self within a participatory and democratic learning process that also allows and encourages the transcendence of self.

(6) We want an end to all forms of war. We want all people exempt from military service. We believe that people should not be forced into military service, while also recognizing that people will protect themselves from violence and attack, by whatever means necessary. In this we support communities' efforts to organize self-defence groups to defend and protect their safety from the violence of the state.

(7)  We want an immediate end to the oppression and victimization of peoples at the hands of the state. We support and struggle with feminism, as well as aboriginal, black, queer, youth, human, and animal liberation struggles, including the valuation of elders. We are anti-ableist, anti-fascist, anti-sexist, anti-racist, anti-ageist, anti-homophobic, anti-speciest, anti-authoritarian, and against neo-liberalism and neo-conservatism. We support the liberation of identity, and the right to self-determination.

(8)  We want freedom for all political prisoners, and a gradual abolition of all prisons, jails, and authoritarian mental-health institutions. We believe that the legal system is neither just, nor representative of the needs and demands of the people. We envision a society that employs community engagement rather than social ostracization in dealing with those most disaffected.

(9)  We want a justice system that resides in the communities it affects, responds to the needs of all within those communities, protects the inalienable human rights of all, and seeks resolution rather than revenge, equality rather than the protection of elite interests. We believe when all parties are represented, equally and fairly, as part of a due democratic process, that conflict resolution, aiming towards consensus, tends to sufficiently resolve crises, and leave all parties content. In this we admire and take as a model a number of aboriginal justice systems.

(10) We want clean air, clean water, free universal access to all forms of media, health care, and public transportation, as well as the ability to produce and consume foods, herbs, and drinks, free of industrial toxins, pesticides, genetic engineering and manipulation. We believe that our environment and our interaction with and within it, determines not only our health and well-being, but our ability to participate as active members of our society.

This basis of unity was influential for a number of organizations that were affiliated with TAO and grew from initial membership with TAO. The statement is repeated in length here because of that influence and because it shows the very real world, material, orientation of anarchist activists online.

Another active group, and one that formed through TAO, has been the May-First/People Link. MayFirst/People Link began life as NYC TAO, as Resist.ca was once TAO Vancouver. MayFirst/People Link (mayfirst.org) identifies itself as a politically-progressive member-run and controlled organization that works to redefine the concept of "Internet Service Provider" in a collective and

collaborative way. This is, like TAO, an attempt to break down the division between producers and users/consumers in a way that helps to make use and/or
service provision mutually educational. Emphasis is placed on knowledge and
skill sharing. MayFirst/People Link's formal members are organizers and activists. In their model of organizing they have collectively chosen to elect a Leadership Committee to maintain operations between meetings and to give some
continuity to organizational practices. They organize internally as a cooperative among active members. These active members s pay dues, buy equipment,
and then share the organizational equipment for websites, email, email lists,
and other active Internet purposes. MayFirst/People Link was targeted by US
federal authorities for a server seizure in 2012.

Another important TAO offshoot has been Resist.ca. Resist has provided
web and e-mail resources for a variety of anarchist and non-authoritarian activist groups and individuals particularly on the West Coast of North America.

Perhaps the most active and widespread organization in the North American context is Riseup Networks (riseup.net). Riseup provides online communication tools for people and groups working explicitly on liberatory social
change. Riseup users are recommended and go through a vetting process to
ensure fit with organizational commitments and mandate. That is, services are
not provided simply as an alternative Gmail for personal use. Instead the emphasis is on providing resources that will be used in actions supporting liberation movements and actions against exploitation and oppression, if broadly
conceived and undertaken. Riseup seeks to create democratic alternatives to
corporate resources and practices self-determination within its collective network by controlling their own secure means of communications. Giving a
sense of the breadth of resources provided by Riseup and the great number of
people who they have supported, their services run more than 10,000 mailing
lists. Riseup runs on more than eight boxes. They also provide regular security
updates to users and actively work to produce new, secure infrastructures.

Riseup has explicitly worked to protect users from surveillance or data capture by the state. Their approach and commitment can be gleaned from a
statement provided to users in response to closures of email providers over
concerns with spying and state breaches of security.

> We would like to clearly state that Riseup has never given any user infor-
> mation to any third party. We have never permitted installation of any
> hardware or software monitoring on any system that we control.
> We will do everything in our power to protect the data of social move-
> ments and activists, short of extended incarceration. We would rather
> pull the plug than submit to repressive surveillance by our government,

or any government. We are doing everything we can, as quickly as possible, to forge forward with options that would prevent us from having to shut down, in case we are faced with making such a decision. In cooperation with other groups, we are hard at work to develop and deploy a radical new infrastructure that would allow us to provide email in a way that is a thousand times more secure and that would prevent us from having access to any user's data. We have been working on this for over a year, but we have a lot more work to do before it is finalized.

These projects of organized anarchy have provided collectively much of the resistance infrastructures relied on by activists over the last two decades. They have maintained services, provided skills and knowledge, organized material spaces and facilitated relationships of solidarity. It is not too much to say that they have provided the communications and networking backbone of movements from the alternative globalization movements, Occupy, and antifascist movements of the present post-Trump world in the global North. Yet they have done so largely in the shadows of popular or mainstream culture. The spotlight has been held by a more famous manifestation, one that effectively combines activism and theater (or more properly perhaps cinema).

### 3     Anonymous

Perhaps the most famous and impactful example of online radical activism, certainly in terms of popular culture, is Anonymous. With their Guy Fawkes masks and cryptic videos these hacktivists have forged a striking image and reputation in contemporary culture and politics. The name Anonymous refers to a decentered, loose affinity group of online activists and hackers. Their decentered structure means that they are largely formless and structureless in reality and practice not only in image. As communications scholar and McGill University Professor Gabriella Coleman suggests: "Anonymous is a little bit hard to define, because it's a collective name that anyone around the world can take" (quoted in Early Edition 2015). Anonymous activists share primarily an action orientation and an identity. They express important shared narrative practices, and symbolism. They hold up a banner that can be adopted by diverse users as needs and circumstances arise (Shantz and Tomblin 2014).

By their very nature as an anonymous grouping that seeks privacy and avoidance of surveillance their members are largely unknown, nameless, unidentifiable. Gabriella Coleman suggests that what is known of the demographics of the grouping situates most of the Anonymous members as youth between the ages of 15 and 35. Almost all of the demographic information known about Anonymous comes from those members who have been arrested, however, so cautions must be taken in drawing hard conclusions. That information might say more about characteristics of the people who are caught than about the broader participant group.

Anonymous activists carry out their activism through a mix of what might be viewed as newer and older tactics from denial of service attacks and hacks to whistleblowing or public shaming. Coleman notes that Anonymous was initially known primarily as a prankster grouping gaining first notoriety for internet pranks. Since 2008 they have turned to direct action and political campaigns, projects, and interventions that are more serious in intent and design. Among the issues Anonymous has become known for advocating involve state or corporate intrusion on privacy, issues of censorship, opposition to surveillance, and matters of free speech.

With the emergence of Black Lives Matter and community movements against police brutality since the police killing of unarmed teenager Michael Brown in Ferguson, Missouri in 2014, Anonymous has actively supported civilians opposing police violence. Operation Ferguson provided resources for protesters speaking out and mobilizing against the racist policing practices of the Ferguson police force responsible for killing Michael Brown. Anonymous has worked to see the names of officers involved in the killing of civilians released publicly. They have also brought attention to disruptive and obstructive police officials and police association representatives who have worked to shield police who kill civilians or who try to blame the victims. Since Ferguson this anti-police brutality work has continued in cases involving police harm to civilians in the United States and Canada.

In terms of online activism Anonymous has been most well-known for DDOS, or distributed denial of service, targeting in which overwhelming traffic is directed to a specific website causing the server to shut down. The site becomes inaccessible as a result. This is a way to shut down an offending institution's online venues and potentially cost time, resources, money, supporters, and/or sponsors. Anonymous has also circulated confidential documents and publicized information in a form of whistleblowing to the public (Shantz and Tomblin 2014).

More recently Anonymous has turned to doxing. This practice has been used to "out" offending individuals by releasing publicly their names and private information such as phone numbers or home addresses. This particular tactic has been used especially in cases of police violence to name relevant officers involved. It should be noted that the impact is usually one of publicity or shaming more than severe consequences for government or corporations. As Coleman suggests: "They don't usually make a call and then do nothing.

Many times they will exaggerate what they will do" (quoted in Early Edition 2015).

In one particularly significant and effective action against Canadian government and security forces Anonymous took responsibility for shutting down the websites of the Canadian Security and Intelligence Service (CSIS), the Canadian government's spy agency. This was done as an appeal for Canadians to oppose Bill C-51, a particularly repressive piece of legislation that became law as the Anti-Terror Act of 2015. The Act contains provisions that give CSIS investigative powers, allows for the criminalization of so-called bad thoughts alone (rather than terrorist actions), and allows for the criminalization of economic activity such as strikes, boycotts, or blockades. The Act also extends possibilities for criminalization of protests, particularly those against energy projects in Canada. The law also gives police additional powers to arrest people pre-emptively, before they have involved in any protest actions.

While primarily viewed as an online phenomenon, activism also occurs in the real, material world, a point that is reinforced by the fact that security forces have killed Anonymous activists. With the RCMP killing of James McIntyre in 2016, Anonymous announced that McIntyre was the fourth of its members to be killed by security forces around the world in four years.

4      Collective Anarchy Online

Online organizing perhaps reflects or plays into the more caricatured notions of anarchism as individual rebellion or disobedience. Anyone can act to the extent of their knowledge, comfort, or expertise in ways that they alone see as most appropriate. And they need have little commitment or accountability toward anyone else. This is sort of an extreme, or ideal type, version of individual liberty. To be sure, practices like Anonymous, floating signifiers that allow anyone who wishes to claim the identity, are emblematic of this form of action. At the same time, there are more accurately identified Anonymous groupings with material associations and interconnections.

Online spaces and projects lend themselves to the sorts of organizing and actions that more closely align with philosophical anarchism. They are also particularly suited to synthesist arrangements in which people with very slight, ethereal connections can align and work together. And ephemeral practices are suited to online activism in which people link and de-link successively as interests, priorities, and projects arise.

It would be a mistake to focus solely or primarily on individualist forms of organizing online (ephemeral, temporary, immaterial, distant) and/or to suggest that this is the extent of online anarchist organization. From the beginning of anarchist involvement in cyberspace (which is really from the very emergence of the public internet itself), anarchist participants have pursued collective actions through material organization. This has included material (real) world, old school, organizing on a face-to-face basis in actual immediate contexts, often in rather traditional forms such as affinity groups, activist collectives, workers' cooperatives, and so on. And it has taken place in physical organizing spaces (in clubs, community centers, anarchist infoshops, etc.).

Very quickly given the nature of the internet, collectives and groupings in diverse and dispersed locales found each other, connected, and federated in networks of organized anarchy. The forms of organization within the federations may have been largely ethereal and online but this is not the entire story. Anarchist collectives online often, and more of than is generally supposed, regularly held, and hold, gatherings and conventions in which members of diverse collectives have travelled to a specific locale to meet, socialize, strategize, and develop their shared organizational capacities.

For years TAO rented an office in a mid-century office building in downtown Toronto, right in the heart of the emerging new technology and media district. Few could have guessed that a thriving anarchist collective held regular meetings in a historic building situated midway between CityTV and the Canadian Broadcasting Corporation (CBC) headquarters. Meetings were held at least once a week with a half dozen, or more, members regularly in attendance. The space was also something of a meeting space and organizing center for local anarchists as well as people involved in campus organizing, anti-poverty movements, and union organizing.

The online work was always viewed as part of broader, and deeply rooted, community organizing. As such TAO workers provided labor and technical education, and insights to numerous local community and workplace movement groups. They also provided logistical support and communications infrastructure for larger mobilizations and actions, including civil disobedience, protests and demonstrations, eviction defense for tenants, housing squats, occupations, anti-deportation defense, and other direct actions. TAO also made equipment available on loan to groups organizing their own actions. In that way they made technology and equipment available to lower income groups that could not have otherwise afforded it. TAO also provided equipment and training to anarchist spaces like the Anarchist Free Space and Free Skool which could not have accessed such material and knowledge otherwise.

Perhaps ironically, the supposedly ephemeral, ethereal realm of online organizing has given rise to very real, material, and relatively durable movement infrastructures. These have in many cases outlived the collectives that produced them in the first place. Many of these infrastructures are now into their second decades, having lasted as long as the public internet itself. And it is not going too far to say that many of these infrastructures have become essential components of anti-capitalist and anti-statist projects without which the projects would not have developed, or not been maintained. One can reference TAO, Riseup, Resist.ca, Indymedia, Media Co-op networks, as only a start.

These infrastructures have provided resources and connectivity for, in some cases, numbers of people well into the tens of thousands. And they have connected people across continents. Many have given rise to multiple original projects, from activist archives to discussion fora, to newsletters to hacking groups and more.

5      Process

At the same time it is less often remarked that the format of online discussion is in many ways anathema to preferred anarchist processes of deliberation and debate. Anarchists generally prefer face-to-face discussion and consensus processes of decision making. The internet, on the contrary, is, by definition, not face-to-face (not physically anyway) and discussion often tends toward monologue and assertion rather than constructive dialogue and consensus.

All of the acknowledged problems of online discussion are perhaps magnified in relation to anarchist organizing practices. Among these problems is the lack of nuance in online discussion and the fact that moods do not come across well over the internet.

Anarchists are particularly attuned to the well-being of participants and go out of their way to facilitate participation and create conditions conducive to active involvement by all members of a group or collective or project. This includes paying attention to inclusive language, and practices of respectful, active listening. It also involves awareness of privilege among speakers (gender, racialization, linguistic, economic, etc.). These are more difficult to pursue online.

Meanings can be easily misinterpreted, moods can be misread or missed completely. Humor is culturally and site specific and may not travel well. Anger can flare and so-called flame wars erupt without warning. Empathy does not come readily.

Cyber anarchist collectives like TAO also consciously work to overcome, or at least address and reduce, the gender division of online practices and the dominance of technical activities by males. Collectives have sought gender parity and collectives like TAO have had equal or greater involvement by women relative to men in their collectives. And women have been active in all regards, whether ideological production, online presence, programming, hacktivism, media work, writing and publishing, space maintenance, or meeting facilitation, etc.

## 6      Beyond Novelty

As the internet becomes more and more a sphere of commercial and state activity, it becomes a crucial realm for anti-statist and anti-capitalist organizers. There is no question, and has not been for some time, that the internet is a central sphere of capitalist development and state surveillance as well as of human social interaction, one of historic consequence. The internet has come gone from being a means of human engagement, a tool, to a form or, an expression of, human engagement itself. The medium is more than the message. It has transcended being mere medium almost entirely. It is now social relation.

From the beginning, while many saw, hopefully, a sphere of unfettered human activity, interaction, and freedom, anarchists saw the internet as a crucial site of social struggle—even before this was sensed by most media analysts and certainly by the public at large. It is in this sense that TAO activists maintained, and expressed publicly in various venues, that the internet does not exist.

Too much popular discussion, and academic analysis alike, has tended to focus on the supposed novelty of online activism. Whether the focus is on Anonymous or earlier manifestations of hacking or Wikileaks or denial of service attacks (DDOS), the emphasis has been overwhelmingly on novelty. While there are, to be sure, novel aspects of online activism (particularly in the reach of tactics, means of hiding identities that might otherwise be criminalized, etc.), much of online activism has direct antecedents in fairly familiar activist repertoires. Anonymous and hacking have antecedents in forms of sabotage. Wikileaks extends and innovates practices of whistleblowing, Denial of service actions represent forms of civil disobedience such as sit ins or blockades.

## 7      Connectivity

What is perhaps most notable and new in the internet is the reach that the internet has given to anarchist organizers and to anarchist ideas more generally. It has, in spread of ideas and actions, provided an unprecedented means for the dissemination, promotion, and, significantly, explanation of anarchist ideas, perspectives, and projects.

It has also opened access, even to longtime anarchists, to heretofore hidden, obscured, inaccessible, forgotten anarchist histories, documents, and ideological products (essays, newspapers, zines, speeches, etc.). It has provided means for sharing anarchist actions and promoting activities. It has also opened important channels for communication and alliance building. The internet has provided a means for bringing together previously far flung anarchist individuals and collectives in ways that allow for acknowledgement, support, solidarity, and concerted action.

It is hard to overestimate the role of the internet in the late twentieth century revival of anarchism in North America. It seems clear though that much of the development of anarchism over the last twenty years is owed to online organizing of various sorts. This is so even at the level of communication alone.

As someone who was active as an anarchist through the 1980s and early 1990s it is impossible to overstate the sense of isolation and detachment that one experienced and felt working on projects in various locales, whether in small towns, like Essex or Kingston, Ontario or in large cities like Vancouver or Toronto.

Communication with anarchists in other areas was confined to information read in limited numbers of small magazines, journals, and zines as well as through correspondence with their publishers and authors. The other source of communication came through occasional meetings with travelers from other areas. Even these latter opportunities were limited if one was not living in areas where there was an existing anarchist space where folks from afar could land, connect with, and meet local anarchists. In the absence of anarchist free spaces, bookshops, or infoshops, isolation could be stark, leaving even local anarchists unknown to each other.

CHAPTER 7

# Beyond Therapy: Autonomist Movements against "Mental Illness"

There is a growing network of anarchist mental health groups across North America and beyond in which people are exploring extreme states of consciousness outside the conventional maps of disease and disorder. These networks seek autonomy from the psy disciplines and their various practitioners, including even restorative therapists. Emphasizing self-determination, participatory decision-making and control by psych survivors themselves, I term these movements *autonomist* to express this focus on autonomy. Autonomist movements attempt to break these hermeneutic circles, providing opportunities for the expression of experiential voices. They provide a context in which the views and experiences of clients or survivors are taken seriously.

For autonomists, "mental illness" diagnoses and various psy practices are social constructions. Survivor and client movements provide spaces for examining those constructions and developing alternative constructions. These spaces can involve actual organizing spaces and resource centers such as the Freedom Center and its numerous workshops or venues and support networks such as the Icarus Group. Autonomist movements also allow survivors to develop their own psychological and social practices based on their own needs and experiences. This contributes, as part of an holistic approach, to survivor self-determination, empowerment and independence, aspects that are central to biopsychosocial recovery models. These concepts of autonomy, interdependence, and mutual aid—that are central to autonomist movements and articulated in projects such as the Freedom Center and the Icarus Project—contribute to the development of broader anti-psychiatry, psych survivor, and mad liberation movements. These movements pose crucial questions regarding what it means to be mad in an insane world, and they create alternatives to coercive systems that currently manage and capitalize on notions of in/sanity. For autonomists, such systems are deeply authoritarian in nature, entrenched in patriarchal, imperialist, capitalist, and ableist relations that serve to generate profit, justify incarceration, and enforce conformity (Dorter 2007). This paper examines autonomist practices through a discussion of the Freedom Center and the Icarus Project.

1        Beyond Therapy: Autonomous Movements and
         Collective Alternatives

Notions of mental illness exist through consensus and persist through convention. Despite programs and relationships that are structured around notions of self-determination, medical and psychological models are alive and
well in recovery programs. Indeed, in many contexts they are still presented as
essential truths, with their disease terminology, pathologizing and deficit-fo-
cus providing the powerful langage of mental illness discourses (Walker 2006,
72). As Walker (2006, 81) suggests, rigid abstractions such as "mental illness"
are "linguistic 'balls and chains' when it comes to helping people become
self-determining."

    Medical and psychological models "position practitioners as expert and
client as more or less passive recipient of 'treatment.' The focus of 'treatment'
is on the elimination of 'symptoms'" (Walker 2006, 74). There is a reliance on
therapists who supposedly have the expertise to help one overcome their
"pathology." Such vocabularies of "expert" and "patient," "treatment" and
"symptoms" are acually creating and reinforcing a particular world and
worldview. They also serve to diminish the experiences and insights of "clients" themselves.

> By seeing the medical and psychological vocabularies as truths (as op-
> posed to perspectives) we cannot see the profoundly destructive conse-
> quences of them. These vocabularies comprise closed conceptual sys-
> tems in which everything can be explained within them (not unlike a
> so-called "delusional" system). Martin Heidegger called these often im-
> penetrable, closed interpretive systems *hermeneutic circles*.
>
> WALKER 2006, 82; EMPHASIS IN ORIGINAL

As Walker (2006, 82) concludes from his years of practice as a therapist: "Equally disturbing is the fact that this 'hermeneutically sealed' conceptual system
keeps us from hearing and taking seriously the emerging voice of the people
we are trying to help (e.g. the Mental Health Consumer Movement)."

    The objectives and values of disabled peoples' organizations and organiza-
tions of users or survivors of mental health services have not always been consistent with consumerism. Such groups have attempted to assert the legitimacy
of experiential knowledge and their status as citizens against official responses
that would identify and construct them as self-interested pressure groups.
Drawing on empirical research involving groups of disabled people and of
mental health service users or survivors, Barnes (1999) identifies the significance

of shared identity as a basis for collective action along with more pragmatic motivations for influencing the character of health care services. Barnes (1999) notes especially the significance of self-organization among the groups discussed.

Self-organizing health movements have helped to transform and overcome "a medical culture that long ago persuaded people that 'health care' is synonymous with what physicians do" (Rosen 1994, 40). Autonomists attempt to create alternative worlds and worldviews, in the here and now of everyday life (rather than in some far off utopian future). Autonomist movements work against the treatment approach by attempting to provide social spaces for the physical and psychological enactment of alternatives. These are spaces and practices of actual self-determination and decision-making by survivors and clients. Rather than an approach that privileges external experts, it is a do-it-yourself (DIY) centered approach to social and psychological life.

Autonomist approaches find an echo in postmodern consultation or postmodern therapy. Such approaches show how language and discursive practices, socially situated in relations of power, construct realities rather than "discovering" them (Walker 2006, 71). Walter and Peller (2000) note the different approach taken by restorative therapists and practitioners of postmodern consultation. There is a shift in perspective regarding the role of clients in the process. Walter and Peller (2000, 32) outline the contours of this shift: "So instead of asking, 'How do we know what is real about the client?' we have decided the more relevant question is 'What do our own clients want and what new ways of speaking and conversing might help?'"

Autonomist movements seek to go beyond the limited reforms of restorative therapy, developing new ways to meet their needs themselves in ways that move outside of individualistic client/consultant-based relationships. As Barnes (1999, 82) notes: "Collective action based in common experiences of oppression, disadvantage or social exclusion should be distinguished from an assertive consumerism which seeks to maximize individual self-interest". Such an analysis makes a distinction between interest-group politics in which relatively powerful lobbies attempt to influence policies in order to reinforce or extend their already strong position and the actions through which groups excluded from power are able to improve their position. These latter actions require collective organization and the development of confidence and skills within both groups and individual members (Barnes 1999, 80).

Movements of survivors, they are interested in helping people, themselves, improve the quality of their lives. Recognizing the social character of mental health, and notions of mental health, they attempt to provide collective support and education, rather than, as is often the case in Western medical approaches, focusing on an individual abstracted from social networks, communities and, even, locales. Mead and MacNeill (2004) and others stress the central importance of client or survivor peer support in improving peoples' life quality. Of course, peer networks and social support are key for anyone's sustained well-being.

Autonomists attempt to provide mutual support networks of people who have experiences with mental health systems. As Barnes (1999, 82) suggests: "This is capacity-building amongst communities of people whose identities have been devalued and who, individually, have been largely powerless to achieve change." Autonomist movements develop new plans for living, challenging taken-for-granted norms and values (Crossley 1999). Many contemporary autonomist movements deploy forms of counter-science, alternative practices for alternative forms and objects of knowledge or expertise. Movements open up new spaces for knowledge production and allow for a body of counter-discourses to develop (Crossley 1999). Many movements attempt to transform society from within, through what Melucci (1986; 1996) terms "laboratories of experience." Such laboratories are heterotopias, or actually existing utopias in which the values and ideals that are central to movements' political projects are embodied and enacted (Crossley 1999). Heterotopias are the "experiments in practice" for the coming communities of mad liberation.

## 2      Freedom Center

Freedom Center was founded in May of 2001 when several people diagnosed with severe mental illness, including schizophrenia, bipolar (manic depression), and obsessive-compulsive disorder, came together in the Pioneer Valley region near Northampton Massachusetts to form the area's first advocacy and support group run by and for mental health consumers and psychiatric survivors themselves. Through Freedom Center they sought to defy stereotypes of helplessness, break the silence around psychiatric abuse, expose the propaganda of pharmaceutical companies and challenging people to stand up against a system that fails to meet their true needs (Freedom Center 2008, n.p.).

Freedom Center is an activist community and organizing space operated by and for people labeled with severe "mental disorders." Their emphasis is on compassion, human rights, self-determination, and holistic options. Through the center psychiatric survivors attempt to alternatives to the mental health system and the despair, abuse, fraudulent science and dangerous treatments often associated with it.

The Freedom Center is one of a collection of grassroots organizations springing up across the country in reaction to the prevalence of medication in America. It alerts people to the downside of psychiatric drugs but does not try to force people off them: it seeks instead to help sufferers find the best methods of coping, even if their solution is unconventional by the standards of the medical establishment.

> *FORBES* 2004, 122

The Stated Goals of the Freedom Center are as follows:
1. to end all force and coercion, including involuntary treatment and forced drugging;
2. to ensure access to resources such as housing is without strings and not conditional on treatment "compliance;"
3. to defend human rights and ensure protective laws and regulations are enforced;
4. to ensure all treatment decisions are based on true informed consent and accurate information about risks;
5. to change drugging as the medical standard of care for psychosis;
6. to end all psych drugging of children and offer alternatives instead;
7. to support effective alternatives such as nutrition, exercise, holistic health care, nature and animals;
8. to provide voluntary, non-paternalistic social supports such as peer-run programs, housing, income, and individual and family therapy;
9. to create Soteria House-style options;
10. to expose psychiatric and pharmaceutical industry myths, propaganda, and corruption;
11. to end wasteful bureaucracies and expensive professional elites;
12. to break the silence around trauma and abuse;
13. to end fear and misunderstanding of "madness" and extreme states of consciousness;
14. and to make common cause with progressive movements for social justice and ecological balance (Freedom Center 2008, n.p.).

Freedom Center invites membership from all who have been labeled with "mental illness," psychiatric abuse survivors, and anyone who experiences extreme mental and emotional states. They also allow participation from allies and supporters but prefer to meet with mental health staff allies prior to granting them membership.

They try to alert people to the serious dangers of psychiatric drugs so that they can make truly informed decisions. While contesting the ways in which the system pushes drugs on people, they support everyone's choice in their own recovery as they define it for themselves. Those who choose to take psychiatric drugs are welcome at Freedom Center. In their words: "We don't judge people...We respect self-determination and choice, and approach all drug use and lifestyle choices from a harm reduction philosophy" (Freedom Center 2008, n.p.).

Freedom Center offers support groups, free yoga classes, and free acupuncture clinics, all of which are provided weekly. The support groups involve approximately 20 people who share stories and resources, discuss recovery strategies and plan educational and advocacy campaigns. The groups are entirely peer organized and provide people opportunities to speak openly about their experiences and share feelings of anger and pain in ways that are not possible in groups organized and run by mental health professionals (Freedom Center 2008, n.p.). Participants attempt to provide effective holistic alternatives and education. In addition they engage in advocacy against coercion and dehumanization, demonstrate against dehumanizing treatment in area psychiatric facilities. They also provide space in which people can support each other in reducing or ending use of psychiatric drugs. Among their broader social change efforts they work to fight against housing discrimination. They are also engaged in public education through speaking engagements discussing their experiences as survivors of psychiatric violence and through a weekly FM radio broadcast featuring interviews with psychiatric survivors and activists.

> Also, we are a mutual aid community of equals, and we ask that everyone who receives any kind of help through the Freedom Center please turn around and help someone else in the future with your time, resources, or a money donation (money donations are always optional). This does not have to be "officially" volunteering with the Freedom Center, it just means that in your life you need to turn around and help others when you've been helped and you're feeling able to do so. That way the whole world gets better.
>
> FREEDOM CENTER 2008, n.p.

The Freedom Center's activist campaigns have made some important gains as well. They have intervened directly to help people avoid hospitalization. They have also worked to match clients with peer advocates to meet with doctors and push for improvements and true choice in their medication. They have assisted clients in pressing human rights complaints and standing up for their rights, while helping to connect clients facing violations with lawyers and resources.

They have educated the broader community on issues of forced drugging with debilitating psych meds, gaining widespread media coverage for their campaigns. They have taken direct action to intervened at a run-down local mental health residency where clients received substandard treatment in violation of the. They have also initiated a reform campaign against upper management policies at ServiceNet, a major local mental health service provider, pushing for changes after hearing several personal stories of abuse and mistreatment. Residents there have reported significant improvements since the protests began.

They have co-sponsored a weekly film series at Mt. Holyoke college with rare documentaries on mental health and the survivors' movement. Their regular "Speak-Outs on Psychiatric Abuse" break the silence and prompt audience members to join in and tell their own stories of mistreatment. They have spoken at college and high school classes, as well as at information tables on the street.

Their work has been recognized through awards from the Smith College social work school graduating class of 2003 and the psychology students association at Mt. Holyoke College.

As Freedom Center participants suggest, their efforts are more than elements of a social reform movement. More broadly they are part of a movement that redefines active citizenship, calling into question markers of inclusion and exclusion from the legitimate political community.

> Our successes show that the time is right for our movement to advance. To live with the label of "severe mental illness" in America is to be condemned to a second class citizenship of life at the margins and the shadows. Our rights are routinely violated by doctors and helping professionals who inflict emotional abuse and physical violence on us in the name of "treatment." Despite the courageous reform efforts begun by mental patients and their supporters in the early 1970s, today people labeled "mentally ill" still face widespread mistreatment, discrimination, and dehumanization. Service agencies routinely treat people in severe emotional distress as if we were criminals or misbehaving children; everyone in the Freedom Center has a story to tell of physical and verbal abuse, coercion, and disrespect.
>
> FREEDOM CENTER 2008, n.p.

Freedom Center places a premium on survivor self-determination and participatory decision-making, in which people are able to structure practices, treatments and supports in ways that address the multifaceted character of their identities, and biological, psychological and social needs. They attempt to address the concern that medical model approaches impede possibilities of recovery: "Instead of effective holistic alternatives and social supports, we are pushed—often against our will and rarely with truly informed consent—to

take toxic medications based on dubious science and with questionable effi-
cacy. The severely debilitating and even brain-damaging side effects often turn
'recovery' into an impossibility" (Freedom Center 2008, n.p.). The search for
self-directed alternatives also drives members of the Icarus Project.

3      The Icarus Project: Navigating the Space between Brilliance and
       Madness

The Icarus Project collective began when two people who had been psychologically labeled met and started touring, sharing their experiences and
sparking dialogue about mental health. Today members of the Icarus collective travel around the US and internationally to help out at community speaking events and discussions, as well as offering skill sharing sessions and trainings. They view their work as "navigating the space between brilliance and
madness."

They have developed much experience with issues such as group facilitation, community organizing, dealing with emotional crisis and extreme states
of consciousness, providing effective emotional support, and conflict resolution. Icarus has also developed peer counseling trainings and trainings on
community organizing for radical mental health.

Participants call for new space and freedom for extreme states of consciousness, and alternatives to the medical model and the traumatic legacy of psychiatric abuse.

> We recognize that we live in a crazy world, and insist that our sensitivi-
> ties, visions, and inspirations are not necessarily symptoms of illness.
> Sometimes breakdown can be the entrance to breakthrough. We call for
> more options in understanding and treating emotional distress, and we
> believe that everyone, regardless of income, should have access to these
> choices.
>
> ICARUS PROJECT 2008, n.p.

The Icarus vision is one that respects diversity and embraces harm reduction
and self-determination around treatment decisions. All psych survivors are
welcome, whether they take psychiatric drugs or not and whether they describe themselves with diagnostic categories or not. Autonomy is a critical
aspect of the Icarus Project and along with mutual aid provides a key organizing principle. In their words: "The Icarus Project is a collaborative, participatory adventure fueled by inspiration and mutual aid. We bring the Icarus vision to reality through a national staff collective and a grassroots network of

autonomous local groups" (Icarus Project 2008, n.p.). Participants sustain local groups through a variety of activities: facilitating a website community, distributing publications, educating the public, offering tools, sharing skills, creating art, engaging in advocacy, enhancing community capacities, offering technical assistance, providing inspiration and solidarity. Within the grassroots network of local groups people gather locally "for listening, education, support, mutual aid, art, activism, access to alternatives, and any creative ventures they can dream up" (Icarus Project 2008, n.p.).

The Icarus project operates on the basis of eight points of unity. They are: beyond the medical model; respect for diversity; self-education about alternatives; anti-oppression/anti-hierarchy; balancing wellness and action; access; non-violence; and transparency. Each point is discussed below.

(1)   Beyond the medical model. While respecting the treatment decisions people make, Icarus participants refuse to define themselves as essentially diseased, disordered, broken, faulty, and existing within the bounds of DSM-IV diagnosis. They are exploring unknown territory and don't steer by the default maps outlined by professionals and pharmaceutical companies. They attempt to draw new maps (Icarus Project 2008, n.p.).

(2)   Respect for diversity. They welcome people who take psych drugs and people who do not, as well as people who use diagnostic labels like "bipolar" to describe themselves and people who do not identify with these terms. They do not exclude people on the basis of politics, lifestyle choice, recreational drug use, "criminal" behavior, or other outsider identities. They understand that participants all have a lot to learn from each other, so they respect each other's choices. As they suggest: "While the current social system and medical model have the tendency to divide us, we want our experiences of madness—as we understand them—to unite us" (Icarus Project 2008, n.p.).

(3)   Self-education about alternatives. Much of what the media, medical establishment, and institutions tell people about "mental illness," psych drugs, and how the diagnosed have to live their lives is not true. Icarus participants educate themselves and others. In their words: "We explore holistic and spiritual approaches to handling our extreme states of consciousness. We learn as much as we can about any medical treatments we are using, and encourage each other to make informed choices. Icarus is a sanctuary for people thinking outside the mainstream and creating their own definitions of health" (Icarus Project 2008, n.p.).

(4)   Anti-oppression/anti-hierarchy. Local groups work to be anti-authoritarian and inclusive. As well time is devoted to working against racism, classism, sexism, homophobia and other oppressive behaviors. As a radical mental

health support network, affiliated groups are expected to create safe and challenging spaces where oppressive behavior is not tolerated.

(5) Balancing wellness and action. Icarus is a place in which people support each other in practicing real self-care. This includes making sure people do not neglect personal basics like food, rest, exercise, and community. People encourage each other to commit to the amount of work they can actually do, and not push themselves past their limits (Icarus Project 2008, n.p.).

(6) Access. In their words: "We don't need more alternatives that only rich people can afford. All Icarus gatherings follow the policy that 'no one is turned away for lack of funds.' We work to create options and choices that are available to all" (Icarus Project 2008, n.p.).

(7) Nonviolence. Participants believe that they will bring about lasting change in the world through dialogue, compassionate listening, mutual aid, and grassroots networks of support. These heterotopic practices may in time form a viable alternative to the current system of government, bureaucracy, domination, and corporate culture.

(8) Transparency. They believe in public access to information about how people are making decisions, spending money, distributing responsibility, and otherwise delegating the work of organizing together.

## 4    Autonomy Movements, Agency and Identity

The mental health or psych survivors movements, as Walker (2006, 76) suggests, have long recognized their struggles "as similar to that of the other marginalized (to use another postmodern term) groups such as women, gay men and lesbians, African Americans, and other minority groups." As for other movements of oppressed groups, autonomous mental health movements or mad liberation groups have worked to shift the identities of participants. They provide a mutually supportive and participatory environment in which people can develop identities and roles beyond being mental health clients.

As Harlene Anderson (1997, 71) suggests:

The dominant voice, the culturally designated professional voice, usually speaks and decides for marginal populations—gender, economic, ethnic, religious, political, and racial minorities—whether therapy is indicated and, if so, which therapy and toward what purpose. Sometimes unwittingly, sometimes knowingly, therapists subjugate or sacrifice a client to the influences of this broader context which is primarily patriarchal, authoritarian and hierarchical.

Theorists of new social movements (Melucci 1985; Crossley 1999; McCally 2002; Day 2005), place the emphasis on agency. In the view of authors such as Melucci and Day, identities are created and re-created through practices within movements rather than through one's "being." New movements are distinguished from old movements, such as economic movements, by shared identities which are constructed and negotiated through repeated processes of "activation" of the social relationships connecting social movement "actors.

Melucci (1985) presents movement goals as primarily symbolic and cultural, emphasizing the meanings emerging through social actions and the ways in which they prefigure future social relations. Cohen (1985) stresses the ways in which new movements make demands on civil society, focusing on the democratization of everyday life through forms of communication and constructions of collective identity. While seeking to democratize the structures through which services are delivered, movements attempt to transform cultural and ideological values in society as a whole rather than solely with health service systems (Barnes 1999, 80).

Theories of new social movements can be particularly helpful in understanding self-organization within pressure groups (Rogers and Pilgrim 1991; Shakespeare 1993). Barnes (1999) finds that new social movement theories provide a helpful framework for distinguishing self-organization from interests groups.

Recently concern has been expressed about "the democratic deficit in the governance of public services," within a context of low levels of people's participation within supposedly democratic processes (Barnes 1999, 74). This concern has influenced studies of social movements as practices by which movements might overcome this deficit.

> Within this context it is particularly pertinent to consider the experiences of those who not only have limited power to exert influence as consumers in welfare markets, but who have also often been excluded from "community." Such exclusions have resulted both from social policies which have been deliberately designed to separate those regarded as deviant or different, and by public attitudes which have reinforced such policies.
>
> BARNES 1999, 74

Barnes (1999) draws on theories of new social movements and new theories of citizenship to identify and discuss two issues that emerge as central for understanding the significance of self-organization among groups who have experienced exclusion, oppression or disadvantage.

Those issues are:

> the significance of identity as a factor defining both motivation to act collectively—to develop groups in which identities can be formed and expressed, and the objectives pursued by such groups; and changes within local governance which have provided space in which user groups can act, but which have prioritized the identity of service users as consumers rather than citizens.
>
> BARNES 1999, 76

Identity within social movements holds both cultural and political significance. Efforts by people to define themselves, rather than submit to a definition imposed by health or welfare professionals, include such diverse practices as direct action and alternative art or activist sociology.

Campbell and Oliver (1996, 105) are exemplary of many social movement theorists in arguing that "transforming both personal and political consciousness is one of the key factors that separates new social movements from the old, more traditional social movements." Disabled people's movements have attempted the redefinition of self through positive imagery while developing a public recognition of disability as oppression (Campbell and Oliver 1996).

## 5    Conclusion

Collaborative and collegial relationships, based on mutual aid and support, replace the paternalistic and hierarchical relations of not only medical approaches but some recovery model practitioners as well. Medical approaches assume that everything must be taught to the client. Autonomists try to get beyond notions that what people already know, through their own day-to-day interactions, is of little use, examining and supporting daily life strategies that are working. These strategies, pursued in an environment of respect, support and experiential understanding, become building blocks for change, both personal as well as social.

Based on the circumstances in which people actually live they can contribute to growing confidence, spurring on other strategies, going beyond medical approaches that view incremental change as insignificant or superficial. Arthur Horvath (2001, 3), of SMART Recovery Incorporated, suggests that the greatest leverage a person has in changing is to focus on that which is most important to herself or himself. This often involves day-to-day activities centered around community and home life. Yet such activities are in many ways sites of struggle and contestation. As Walker (2006, 82) notes, the "normal ups and downs of working or being in relationships quickly get pathologized... A problem with managing work tasks or a pang of jealousy in a relationship is quickly referenced back to a 'mental illness'." They can become reinforcements for psychological models divorced from the social and biological aspects of everyday life.

> The result: many so-called "mentally ill" people have skills and resource-fulness that go unnoticed and therefore uncapitalized on. The skills of negotiating the public transit system, living off welfare (in California about 250 dollars plus food stamps per month), adapting to often danger-ous and unhealthful living conditions, negotiating the bewildering and often unfair social service and child protective agencies, coping with the "mental illness" stigma and ostracization, dealing with being "infan-tilized" (treated as a child or infant by others), struggling with being pathologized by helping professionals, coping with being manipulated and taken advantage of by family members, and developing a whole array of "street smarts"—are all barely noticed behind the "mountain" of pa-thology "heaped" upon them from the medical and psychological per-spectives. Often their quite understandable reactions to so many of these challenges get thrown into the "symptom list" which adds support to "the diagnosis," which implies an inherent and internal "pathology"—all of which contributes to feelings of shame, humiliation and self-blame. The "iron-grip" of these pathologizing discourses causes us to rarely suffi-ciently consider a client's life circumstances when the pathologizing la-bels are applied.
>
> WALKER 2006, 78

The psychological, biological and social are intricately interconnected, espe-cially so for people who are already experiencing marginalization, poverty or isolation. As Harrop, Trower and Mitchell (1996) note, mind and behavior equally influence physiology. Autonomists help each other in removing barri-ers to housing, financial stability, employment and education. This is done through collaborative practices, skill sharing and resource sharing. It includes free schools, communal housing and childcare, craft workshops, apprentice-ships and co-operative, worker controlled workplaces.

These practices are undertaken in environments liberated from the language of psychology and medicine. Autonomists ask each other to focus on things that are rendered obscure of invisible within medical approaches to "mental illness," including independence, participant goals and self-determination.

As Freedom Center and Icarus Project participants are aware, the movement for human rights in mental health is growing internationally. As activists
they are strongly committed to nonviolence. Freedom Center also recognizes
that psychiatrists, nurses, and mental health staff are often trapped in ignorance or bureaucracies, and they try to reach out to the people on the "other
side" with compassion and an attempt to get them to understand and join
them.

> Respect for our opponents—who are often also suffering—is essential.
> We welcome the growing number of mental health professionals, coun-
> selors, staff and system employees who are becoming allies and working
> with us towards common goals—people in the system are often op-
> pressed as well. We believe in directly challenging abuse and advocating
> against institutional power, as well as educating the public, as means for
> change.
> FREEDOM CENTER 2008, n.p.

In response to the question of whether or not they are a radical group, Freedom Center participants note that psychiatry and the mental health system
have become deeply entrenched socially and economically. To speak the truth
and challenge basic assumptions means being treated as though you are too
radical. Many survivors are legitimately quite angry about how the system has
treated them. Many are deeply frustrated "at the widespread hypocrisy of a
helping profession, including psychotherapy, that rarely utters a word about
the violence of involuntary treatment, restraints, medication side effects, elec-
troshock therapy, and degrading labels" (Freedom Center 2008, n.p.). As Freedom Center notes, too often survivors are met with words of understanding
and pity, followed by inaction. Too often they are told that they are angry because they are "crazy" or "unreasonable." Their anger becomes yet another sign
that they are emotional or irrational, politically unstable. Freedom Center
works to oppose such dismissive approaches, in which people's experiences
and analyses are diminished or devalued, to encourage people to learn to vali-
date, respect, and listen to the experiences of survivors and clients.

# CHAPTER 8

# Duty of Care: Anarchist Organizing for Health

It has often been asked, sometimes sneeringly by critics and sometimes in an act of self-criticism by anarchists, "Where are the anarchist doctors?" And there is a real lack or absence identified in this question. Anarchists have started far more bookstores than clinics. They have done more work educating and agitating than in healing and health care.

And this is not entirely surprising. A do-it-yourself ethos only goes so far in terms of medical training and experience within the current structure of hierarchical education and social service bureaucracy, and especially given the costs and legal frame works associated with training the trainers. Given that anarchism is a movement of mostly working class people in a system that charges enormous fees for medical school tuitions it is not a mystery that few will acquire the needed medical skills to start teaching others on a range of necessary medical practices. So too must be considered the costs associated with medical equipment and facilities. At the same time the current system also applies pressures on medical school graduates to operate in specific, privatized ways.

While recognizing these challenges it can be recognized that anarchists have done much to contribute to *preventative* measures to maintain health in anarchist communities. And this includes, as discussed earlier, helping with mental health care and well-being and providing solidarity and mutual aid that can help to reduce stress and stress related illnesses. And anarchists have organized to teach diet and nutrition and herbal treatments and other natural health care aids (within broader health care and wellness practices, including dietary improvements, etc.) as well as healthy approaches to community care and mutual aid.

Beyond this there have been important organizing projects among anarchists to provide health care and medical assistance within working class and poor communities and among activist circles and resistance mobilizations. Most notable among these (in terms of frequency, breadth, and influence) are street medics, many of whom are explicitly influenced by, and informed by, anarchist principles. Many of whom self-identify as anarchists.

## 1    Do-It-Ourselves Healthcare

The DIY (do-it-yourself) ethos is characteristic of anarchist approaches, though many anarchists prefer to call it do-it-ourselves to emphasize the collective, rather than individualized, nature of their efforts. This DIY or DIO emphasis is not surprising given anarchists' disdain for the state and their desire to organize social life and its important elements without a state—against and beyond states. Notably, as anarchists emphasize, this is a very human impulse, particularly where it comes to issues of care, support, health—looking after one another in times of need.

As sociological anarchists like Colin Ward have pointed out repeatedly, under conditions of capitalist privatization and unequal distribution of necessities of life, many people in advanced capitalist societies like those in Canada, the United States, and the United Kingdom are only able to survive and meet their essential needs because of the mutual aid, sharing activities of friends, loved ones, and neighbors.

Much of caring work, in the home and in the community is done on a mutual aid basis, on conditions of sharing rather than sale for profit. This includes child care, elder care, comfort and compassion during times of illness and emergency. And it must be noted too that given the capitalist labor market and the division of labor, most of this work is gendered and done on the basis of women's labors.

Anarchists argue that in the absence of forced labor economies, where one is made to work to produce surplus value for owners of industry and services, people would be freed up to do caring work in the service of their families and communities and would have vastly more time to meet real personal needs rather than working to make owners and bosses wealthy. And this too would allow for a reorganization of labor time and overcoming the gendered division of labor. But that too must be specifically organized toward.

## 2    Holistic Health

Anarchism takes a more holistic and integrated approach to health and wellbeing. So anarchist organizing around issues of health involves fostering and growing healthy social relations. This can include literally growing healthy organic foods. It can also involve wellness techniques and practices, including meditation, yoga, stress reduction, etc. There is also a sense of community contribution to collective and individual wellbeing.

This is not to say that this always plays out in practice. There are uncaring people in anarchist circles and jerkish, unhealthy, behavior and toxic relationships.

And people still have to work or go to school and are rushed and stressed and eat junk food. But anarchists try to organize spaces and resources, and practices that contribute to betterment of health and wellbeing within this.

Anarchist philosophy meets conservationist ethics and preventative approaches. Anarchists maintain that basic healthcare is not difficult to teach or to learn. Exploitation and oppression cause poor health and associated stresses on the mind and body. Yet this is rarely recognized or addressed with mainstream medicalized approaches to health care. People are blamed for experiencing or acting on stress and manipulated to adapt themselves to stressful social structures, systems, and conditions.

Anarchists have challenged and confronted the sources of stress and unhealthy in statist, capitalist social systems. They have also worked to provide some tools to help people care for themselves while changing social structures.

At the Anarchist Free Space in Toronto people ran classes on herbal medicine. There were also regular yoga and meditation sessions. At anarchist bookfairs there have been workshops on local herbs in the wild and on local edible flowers and mushrooms. There have also been workshops on edibles within the local urban environment. These are part of holistic approaches to health that have the benefit of providing access to and information about low cost or free options of locally appropriate and available healthy foods. They are not cures. They are resources.

Anarchists also do much work on community gardening to provide healthy, low cost foods within urban settings, especially for people who generally cannot afford higher priced healthy options, such as organic foods, on a regular basis. Many free spaces have gardens on site in order to provide healthy, nutritious, foods. And many use the vegetables grown to prepare healthy meals to members and the community more broadly on at least a weekly basis. Some free schools teach practices like canning and food preservation that are becoming lost or forgotten arts but which allow for access to healthier foods on a year round basis.

There have been trained doctors and nurses involved in anarchist projects in various local contexts. And there are doctors and nurses contributing to social struggles in various ways, often without fanfare or notoriety.

## 3      Street Medics

Among the most interesting and promising forms of anarchistic health care and health care provision has been the development of street medics. Street medics typically or most commonly provide medical support during protests and street mobilizations. They often provide emergency assistance to people who have been assaulted by police or vigilantes (such as white supremacists or fascists). The rise and networking of street medics on a national and international basis in the United States and Canada was spurred by the police violence unleashed against protesters of a wide range of backgrounds during the mass street demonstrations against the World Trade Organization meetings in Seattle in 1999, at the so-called Battle of Seattle.

With the rise of the fascist Right in the United States over the last few years and their growing confidence, even brashness, about gathering out in the open, especially since the 2016 election that resulted in Trump's election, street medic collectives have played important parts in supporting anarchist and ANTIFA activists in a range of open confrontations in which fascists have attacked with extreme violence. The dual nature of violence at mobilizations around fascists and the violence directed at ANTIFA from both fascists and police makes organized medical support even more essential and pressing.

Anarchist knowledge sharing around health care issues has seen a tremendous spread of knowledge among activists about self-protection at demonstrations. Expectation of tear gas and/or pepper spray has led to wide information sharing about substances to address the use of those noxious substances by police. Activists come prepared with bandanas soaked in vinegar, water bottles, etc.

This all relates to the awareness that even if you are not involved in illegalized or direct action activities you will be attacked by police. The police are not there to stop illegal protests or illegal protest activities, as they might claim, but rather to stomp out dissent, plain and simple.

Anarchist street medics adopt the affinity group structure in protest actions. Street medics act in a buddy system on the streets. That is, they always have at least one other buddy with them when they work. This allows for self-care and protection amongst themselves on the streets in often chaotic circumstances. It keeps people safe and aware under often heated and dangerous situations of police or vigilante assault. It is protective and allows for more effective action.

Another significant aspect of this partnered work model is that it provides some accountability and review of best practices. Supportive debriefing is part of important self-care work that allows medics to look after each other and themselves. This is crucial given the typically high stress context of actions in which street medics are involved.

At the same time they identify themselves as medics publicly so people in need of help or support can find them in a crowd during situations that are potentially marked by stress and/or panic. And they do not engage in more traditionally identified protest or direct action. They maintain a position of aid, assistance and support. They do not openly challenge opponents and they do not act in a provocative manner.

They have generally had some form of formal training and some are trained physicians. Most would have the skills of Emergency Medical Team personnel or paramedics. Street medic training involves around 20 or so hours of training. There are also, in addition to street medic trainings, bridge trainings, a shorter course for people who already have some medical training.

Training as offered through Rosehip Medics in Portland, Oregon, offers skill sets and practical knowledge applicable to street protest and resistance settings. This includes practices not part of formal nurse training, for example. It also goes beyond strictly medical training to include practices of de-escalation and effective interactions with traditional emergency response systems. Basic first aid and CPR courses are offered at many community centers in cities across Turtle Island. And these can be useful. But they do not cover issues of consent, assessments, or detailing reports to give emergency medical service personnel if the person in need of care is transferred from the care of the street medic.

Issues can include dealing with heat stroke and dehydration which come up on long marches. Other issues can include warmth and body temperature in colder settings. In protest situations issues arise with allergic reactions. In terms of supplies—water is key. Liquid Antacid Water (LAW) and/or water in clean and not previously used squirt bottles are key staples. Other supplies include nitrite or vinyl gloves and bandages and band-aids.

Some basic practice includes things like carrying epipens that anyone at a demonstration could do and be trained in using properly. Similarly, do-it-ourselves responses to the opioid and overdose epidemics have more and more people carrying and trained to use naloxone as a life saving measure. This knowledge development has really broken down hierarchies between experts and non-experts and has literally saved thousands of lives.

With the rise of fascist brownshirt groups and real possibilities of extreme violence against ANTIFA and other counter-protesters, street medics have had to prepare for treating serious open wounds, like stab wounds, open lacerations, etc. Fascists have been known to stab people with picket signs and flag poles during demonstrations. The threat is real. This reality means medics have to be ready and prepared for concerns like blood contamination. In addition to nitrite gloves the needs for equipment under such circumstances include goggles, sterile gauze, and sterile padding. People need training in the use of QuikClot and cayenne for issues of more severe bleeding.

Anarchists recognize that in the absence of full blown anarchist based or anarchist friendly alternative medical systems and until those resources are

developed the main work to assist people is often interacting properly and effectively with formal Emergency Medical Systems (EMS). This can include
prepping people for transport and formal levels of advanced care.

Street medics operate within their own Scope of Practice—the scope of activities that they have been trained to carry out. Medics also operate under a
regime of serious consent. This informs all of their actions. They do not touch
people without consent. They consult with people before taking actions and
check in with them as they go along. They respect any "No." This is important
in cases where, for a range of legitimate reasons, people may not want to be
transferred to EMS care.

## 4      Street Medic Organizations

Some medics have formed more durable or "permanent" groups, acting beyond protests and demonstrations. They do training for new medics, educate
members of their communities on various health care and self-care initiatives
and practices and provide some basic health care services in communities.

These developing forms can provide the basis for broader medical services.
And the skill sharing and community based models and approaches expand
and extend knowledge among the community rather than keeping it solely as
the purview of medical "experts."

The key point in this perhaps is that non-experts—regular people acting
out of love, support, and care—are learning these skills. And teaching others.
And putting them into real world, lifesaving, practice. There has been an incredible development of knowledge and sharing of skills over the last two decades coming from explicit need (real experiences in street protests and in
community care) and the desire to care for one another rather than wait for
experts or authorities to do it for them. And it has tapped into a real, deep desire *to know* how to provide and support health care among regular folks who
never saw themselves as a being or becoming doctors or nurses.

This is the power of do-it-ourselves and anarchic organizing. Taking information, knowledge, and experiences and developing them collectively in supportive and caring ways with other regular folks on a non-authoritarian and
non-hierarchical basis of egalitarian knowledge sharing. What some now refer
to as peer-to-peer knowledge and training.

There are street medic organizations active in cities across Turtle Island,
especially in urban centers, of course, but, significantly, not exclusively. Medic organizations also share knowledge and experience with other groupings
and often travel to put on workshops in areas where there are no street medic

collectives, including more isolated areas, to expand knowledge and resources but also to build capacities in as many places as possible. This is a possible community health care structure in formation.

The Albuquerque Black Cross Health Collective is an active grouping of street medics in Albuquerque, New Mexico. They have provided health care assistance during political actions since 2011. They have broadened to provide some health services in surrounding communities outside of the city.

Mutual Aid Street Medics (MASM) have been active in the eastern United States. They provided medical support, street medic trainings and operated a wellness center during the protests against the G20 meetings in Pittsburgh in 2009 (when they were formed). The Mutual Aid Street Medics have done trainings on street medic work, disaster workshops, herbal first aid, and wellness support. Their work has been foundational in spreading street medics practice across North America.

Atlanta Resistance Medics (ARM) began as a loose grouping of people working as the medical committee of Occupy Atlanta. They operated a medical tent around the clock and did first aid trainings. ARM was founded on November 20, 2011, following a weekend long training session provided by Mutual Aid Street Medics. They looked to work autonomously from Occupy and to maintain operations beyond the lifespan of the Occupy camp. They organized and worked according to consensus based and non-hierarchical principles and practices. ARM formally ended operations, as ARM, in 2013.

One particularly active group, and one with an interesting history of organizing work in Canada, was the Activist Health Collective of Ottawa (AHCO). AHCO emerged out of the massive repression of the FTAA meetings in Quebec City in 2001 (the events where I experienced my own tear gas pain and rescue by unionists and street medics). There the police fired thousands of rounds of tear gas into crowds of protesters and residents over the course of a weekend protecting the interests of global capital. The deployment of tear gas by police was so extreme that the Quebec City FTAA operations were given the colloquial designation of "The Tear Gas Holiday" by protesters and the public.

Some activists from Ottawa formed AHCO after participating in a 24 hour training provided by BALM. After providing medical support during a few smaller local actions they requested that BALM come to Ottawa for a training of some 30 people from across North America who wanted to learn about and prepare as street medics. This training was done in preparation for the upcoming G20 meetings scheduled for Ottawa in 2002.

During the G20 protests about 33 people were treated for a range of injuries inflicted by rampaging Ottawa Police Service officers. People suffered dog bites, several concussions, respiratory and other injuries from tear gas and pepper spray, numerous cuts and contusions, and one broken fibula from a rubber bullet fired by police. AHCO made a public campaign around what had happened to people and publicized the police brutality and its effects on victims. This contributed to the Ottawa Police Service being reprimanded.

AHCO would have their next large scale actions during the Take Back the Capital demonstrations of June 26 and 27, 2002. Those protests saw 50,000 people take to the streets against government support for global capital and against austerity programs at home during the G8 meetings in Canada.

The mobilizations would see the opening of the Seven Year Squat against homelessness and housing policy. AHCO members provided health care and medical aid in the squat which included being behind barricades at night. The squat was raided after seven days and brutally evicted by Ottawa police. So much tear gas was used to drive squatters out that the building could no longer be used.

Twenty-two people were charged. Seventeen had charges dropped after signing what amounted to apologies. Five faced trial for indictable offenses (the equivalent of felony charges in the United States) but the judge dismissed the case.

The Black Cross Collective in Portland, Oregon started up following the Battle of Seattle. It worked to attend to the specific health care needs of people engaged in radical actions. The Black Cross Collective was made up of nurses, nurse practitioners, emergency medical technicians, and clinical herbalists. They carried out street medic training sessions in places all along the West Coast, including in Vancouver, British Columbia, Seattle, Olympia, and Eugene. They also set up and offered health services at temporary clinics.

Gateway Region Action Medics (GRAM) was formed in October of 2014 in the context of the police violence inflicted on protesters opposing the racist actions of police in Ferguson, Missouri, particularly the events involving the police shooting of unarmed Black teenager Michael Brown and the rising Black Lives Matter movements against police violence in Ferguson. The GRAM collective has done health care trainings in the area as well.

The Boston Area Liberation Medic (BALM) was founded in Boston in 2001. They describe themselves as an all-volunteer, non-hierarchical, consensus-run organization. They state that there aims have been to provide medical support, by all means at their individual and collective disposal, during progressive demonstrations and direct actions. They have also been oriented toward facilitating the dissemination of medical knowledge. These are all components of empowering progressive communities and struggles as they see it. They have affirmed the importance of diversity in both their own organization and work and in the larger struggles against oppression.

The BALM members have varying levels of medical training and street medic experience and worked with several different health and healing approaches. They have offered the following health-related services to the progressive communities:

> On-site health care support at progressive demonstrations. This includes clinic staff as well as medics on the street.
> We provided and helped coordinate street medic coverage for the 2004 Democratic National Convention in Boston. We also went to the FTAA protests in Miami in 2003, and have attended other large demonstrations on the East Coast. We will continue to cover political actions and related events as they occur.
> Talks and classes for activists on health, street first aid, and related topics. We have given numerous health and safety classes and talks to activists preparing for demonstrations, civil disobedience, direct actions, and peacekeeping activities in other countries. We also sponsor street medic courses and special classes on related topics such as herbal healing. [...]
> Free health clinics for progressive causes. BALM Squad members and their colleagues organized and staffed free health clinics for janitors and their families during the Justice for Janitors strike in the Fall of 2002.
> Health care-related political actions. As street medics, we are concerned about access to adequate and affordable health care, both on and off the streets. Therefore, we plan to take part in political actions that are related to improving public health care.
> BALM

Street medics are active outside of urban areas as well. Appalachian Medical Solidarity (formerly Katuah Medics) is active in southern Appalachia. They have provided medical support at Mountain Justice training camps and at anti-mountain top removal (that is, mining) actions. They have worked with direct action anarchist influenced radical ecology group Earth First! In this regard. They have more recently done work supporting anti-Klan and anti-fascist organizing in areas around southeastern Appalachia. They also do medical and Wilderness First Responder training.

Seven Cities Medic Collective was started as recently as August 2017. They provide medical care at protests around Hampton Roads, Virginia, These efforts are increasingly important with the open rise of the fascist Right and white supremacists in many parts of the United States, which includes mobilizations in the southern US and in rural areas.

5        Holistic Training beyond the Streets

Rosehip Medic Collective offers a 20-hour Community Medic Training. They present this as a sort of advanced first aid course for those that are looking to be resources within communities that generally feel unable to access or unsafe accessing "mainstream" primary and emergency healthcare services.

In keeping with an anarchistic approach, they design the training to be holistic. It involves components that focus on prevention, responding to emergencies, and aftercare. But they also address ways in which people can effectively navigate the complexity and even dangerous procedures of healthcare services. It is expected that participants in the training will leave with a range of useful tools. This knowledge will be helpful whether they are seeking basic first aid knowledge or are looking to help their family members and neighbors. It will, of course, be of use to them if they plan on serving as a medic at a direct action or demonstration, but it is not limited to applicability in such actions.

The curriculum for the Rosehip training pursues a primarily allopathic/ Western biomedical tradition of healthcare. At the same time it involves understandings and practices from other health care other traditions. These include herbal remedies, acupuncture, breathing, etc. The collective notes that in many cases these practices might be much more accessible or effective for many people.

The schedule for the Rosehip training is intensive. There is one evening session and two long days that include a combination of hands-on practices and realistic scenarios so that people are prepared not to panic in the moment of a crisis situation when things move quickly. They seek and work to ensure that their trainings are accessible, safe, and supportive for all participants. They endeavor to work with participants beforehand to ensure that their needs are met and questions answered as much as possible.

They note that this training is distinct from a street medic training, while much core curriculum is the same. Those who want to pursue street medic are provided the opportunity for a brief training that covers some essential like pepper spray and other protest specific issues during an additional session.

The Rosehip curriculum is instructive. It includes:
- the why's, what's, how's and ethics of community medicking
- patient assessment, prevention, basic first aid skills and life-saving techniques
- when and how to access Emergency Medical Services
- emotional first aid, peer mental health support, and advocacy
- packing your first aid kit (rosehipmedics.org).

The training is carried out in Portland.

## 6     Harm Reduction

In the present crisis period of opioid overdoses and deaths, this mutual aid, caring, and sharing approach to health care has been put on vivid display with life altering and society altering results. These include the DIY spaces created by volunteers to allow for safer drug use and overdose prevention. People, of their own time and their own resources have created temporary structures, often under threat of criminalization, to provide necessary supports to people consuming drugs in order to save lives. Far from being formal and officially sanctioned sites, these self-organized spaces are often subjected to harassment by government representatives and police alike.

Notably, states at all levels of politics in Canada and the United States have persisted in their commitment to foolish and fatal (and discriminatory and mean spirited) "drug war" prohibitionist policies that prioritize policing and punishment (and vengeance) over care, compassion, and health. Few government resources relatively have, still been deployed and directed to meet the needs of drug users by governments. Even as these are public and social resources.

Instead, in many diverse areas, the most significant responses to the overdose crises have been volunteer, mutual aid overdose prevention sites and safer consumption sites developed and resourced by regular folks, many of whom are experiential drug users and have that as their "professional training."

Overdose prevention sites and supervised injection sites are often put together on a very "bare bones" basis and can involve little more than a tent in terms of physical infrastructure. Table, chairs, basic shelves, etc. round things out. These are stocked with a range of medical supplies and are equipped to deal with potential overdoses. Food, beverages, and snacks are provided. Much of these supplies are, like the labor, donated by people who support the sites and the work being done within them.

These sites have been run on an illegal or criminalized basis. Many face harassment by vigilantes, police, and bylaw enforcement officers. Many are outright criminalized. Yet on a mutual aid, DIY, self-directed basis they save lives.

These are not necessarily explicitly anarchist projects. Yet they are anarchic or anarchistic in character. And they show the rightness of anarchist approaches to social care and the viability of those approaches on a larger scale and even in unfavorable conditions of crisis and despair. They draw upon the sentiments, even instincts, of mutual aid and solidarity that anarchists have always emphasized as the real glue that holds societies together (rather than cops, courts, and corrections). They show the creative organizing approaches that regular people can take to addressing and alleviating social problems in our communities. They show too the negative role played by states seeking to clamp down on self-organizing even where the actions of the state cost people lives.

Anarchists also emphasize the educational part played by self-organizing activities. When we do it ourselves we learn and we learn how to teach others. These projects have also led to a great dissemination of knowledge about drug consumption and safety as well as health care practices. For example, they have contributed to the distribution of naloxone kits (to address fentanyl overdoses, for example) and the increased knowledge of regular community members in using them properly. The division between experts and non-experts is overcome because people learn, teach each other, and spread expertise. The non-experts become experts.

This has led to a horizontal spread of health care knowledge, awareness, and practice in communities beyond the purview of health care professionals. And these are often marginalized, oppressed, communities that are patronized by government officials and health care experts alike. This horizontalism in anarchism in action. And it shows how DIY health care can and does spread on important issues and leads to an increase in social, as well as individual, knowledge.

It also initiates public knowledge on issues more broadly (helping people to see drug use as a health issue rather than a criminal justice one, for example). And it makes people engaged, proactive actors rather than passive observers or so-called patients.

The Indiana Recovery Program is a participant based and driven association of drug users caring for drug users to end the stigma that harms people and to provide safer conditions for use. They operate a needle exchange program that has been targeted by Indiana politicians and was actually shut down by authorities in 2017. They work to end criminalization of drug use and take a harm reduction approach based on the needs and concerns of users. They emphasize "non-judgemental, participatory and collaborative harm reduction" (IRP website). They have ensured at least 500 overdose reversals.

Overdose Prevention Ottawa touched upon the relations of mutual aid and trust driving, and built through, their work. They also express the frustrations of contexts maintained by prohibitionist governments. Their statement reads, in part:

> Overdose Prevention Ottawa provided the first public safe space in our city for people to use drugs, primarily through injection and inhalation. At that time, there were no harm reduction services that provided a space for people to safely consume drugs. We have built relationships of trust

with people, the building blocks of healing deep wounds. Every day, our guests tell us that they and their friends are alive because of our services.

In just over two months, we have accomplished much to make our city safer for people who use drugs, to combat stigma and criminalization, and fix some of the many gaps in the healthcare system. For 74 days, we have operated without any support from any level of government. It is only through the tireless efforts of our more than 200 volunteers, and through the donations of thousands of private supporters were we able to stand up where our government had failed so many. It is shameful that so many individuals have had to sacrifice so much to fix that failing. But it is also truly inspiring to see the love, the compassion, and unwavering support of our neighbours in the face of this emergency. We have created a powerful community of advocates and we will continue to use that strength to both demand and actively build a better city for everyone.

OPO 017

On the whole, the impacts of these projects have been, without overstatement, remarkable. As but a couple of examples. In Ottawa, Overdose Prevention Ottawa recorded 3445 visits, 5 overdose reversals with naloxone, and hundreds more though other means. In Toronto, similarly, the Moss Park Overdose Prevention Site reversed 106 overdoses in a period of only three months. Their first three months of existence in 2017. They rely on 175 volunteers. In Vancouver at the Overdose Prevention Society the numbers are staggering, and amazing. In under a year, between December 2016 and October 2017, they reported 108804 visits. There were 255 overdoses. And zero deaths.

## 7    A Social War Crime: Targeting the Medics

Police, acting in their customarily unprincipled fashion have taken to identifying medics at the start of demonstrations in order to target them for repression during the clampdown of protests. This despite the fact that medics do not participate in offensive oriented activities during demonstrations and are purely defensive and care oriented throughout. The police targeting is a means to punish protesters and inflict extra harm on activist communities while repressing protest and resistance. Of course the targeting of medics is supposed to be off limits in conflict situations (and viewed as a war crime).

During the June 15, 2000, protest in Toronto against state policies that were harmful, even lethal, to homeless people in Ontario, which was attacked by police and erupted in a full scale police riot, police were particularly vicious toward street medics and injured protesters, many of whom had been seriously injured in a police attack that included police trampling people with riot horses and clubbing people from the backs of moving horses. Many of the people targeted by police already had mobility issues due to illness and ill health from being homeless for years and/or were elderly with mobility issues or failing health.

Toronto medics, many of whom were long time street nurses with years of experience providing health services to poor and homeless people had set up a marked "treatment area" to help people with injuries or who were dehydrated, etc. on a hot summer day. Police drove their horses through the medics' treatment area, clubbing and trampling people who lay injured getting treatment. As well, police directed baton charges against the street medics who were working to heal injured, tired, and/or ill people.

Notably, the medics' treatment area was in a distinct location on the lawn of the provincial legislature (site of a park near government buildings), clearly marked and away from the heart of the protest area where the police riot was in full swing (pun not intended). Police, thus, diverted time resources, and attention away from breaking up the protest, if that was their concern, and instead deployed them solely on the punitive and sadistic basis of inflicting harm on injured people, who were no protesting and could not protest, and their nurses in the process of providing medical care that was in many cases desperately needed.

People hurt by police that day suffered serious injuries, including broken bones and concussions. Tellingly, at one point a street nurse, the longtime anti-poverty advocate Cathy Crowe, tried to get an ambulance to the treatment area to transport a particularly severely injured person to a local hospital only to have the police intervene to stop the ambulance, prevent it from accessing the patient who lay in peril, and turning it around to go back to the hospital empty. Police also, it might be noted, went to local hospitals to arrest people even as they lay in hospital beds bleeding, bandaged, and unconscious.

## 8    Toward Healthy Anarchy

Anarchists maintain that there is much that can be done to raise health care awareness, skills, and practices broadly throughout communities of the exploited and oppressed. First aid and home care can be taught to anyone and provide some initial basic provisions.

At a basic level healthcare should be non-profit, non-harmful, and egalitarian. The sharing of knowledge as a commons would also be applied to medicine and the breaking of pharmaceutical monopolies and their dominance within a constructed scarcity market.

One might expect that in a period of intensified social struggle there will be members of the working class who will come forward to side with and support anarchists, who will have some medical training. This could include the numerous working class people trained as medics within military contexts who have left the military after discharge and who have been radicalized by their experiences (including with the mistreatment of veterans). One cannot overlook the role of medics in other conflicts in the twentieth century who sided with revolutionaries.

The DIY medical ethos has taken on a central and growing importance in recent years. And some of this has been spurred by the DIY examples and experiences of street medics. Perhaps most notable and significant among these are the DIY safe drug consumption sites and supervised injection sites that have been set up in response to the opioid crisis. These practices have been undertaken without sanction or recognition by the law and/or without support from the state—in true anarchist fashion they have put human need and care above respect for or adherence to paper laws or state permission or support. And without concern for profit or even the personal costs borne by the DIY health care providers.

In the twenty-first century many in North America insist on informed involvement in their own health care. Many seek preventative approaches and healthy choices as much as possible. And many seek to play an active role in addressing their own health concerns. This is not a substitute for advanced health care but it does suggest that an appetite for involvement in health care is pervasive and people are not satisfied to leave decisions and knowledge strictly in the realm of professionals. Decentralized technologies and knowledge networks that are part of the current mode of production contribute to this and questions are posed about the extent to which these can be taken over, democratized, and more broadly distributed.

# CHAPTER 9

# Out Here for You: Anarchist Prisoner Defense

There is a famous slogan of the Industrial Workers of the World. It states "You're in there for us, we're out here for you." The slogan is emblazoned on posters, buttons, artwork alongside the image of a prisoner behind bars. This statement is a strong assertion of the responsibility that movements have to fight for prisoners of the struggle, those who have been targeted and captured by the state for their part in social resistance.

This commitment to struggle with and for political prisoners has been an important part of anarchist and syndicalist movements historically. The IWW developed a General Defense Committee specifically to maintain relations of solidarity with and to fight along with movement comrades who have been captured and detained.

Many anarchists consider *all* prisoners as political in an exploitative class system based on private ownership and control of the necessities of life. Thus many anarchists do not differentiate, as some groups like Amnesty International do, between prisoners who have engaged in violent or illegal activities (as defined by the state and its criminal justice apparatuses). Anarchists recognize, first, that states determine these categories (violence/non-violence, legal/illegal, etc.) in unequal and unjust, often arbitrary, ways designed to protect the status quo of inequality and oppression (as in the criminalization of survival strategies of the poor like sex work, shoplifting, panhandling, low level drug sales, binning, etc.) rather than severely harmful activities like workplace deaths, war, or exploitation. Secondly, anarchists point out that state violence is greater than all of the street crime related violence combined but these activities are rarely, if ever, criminalized. Elite deviance is more impactful, more violent, and imposes greater personal, social, and financial costs, in magnitudes greater than street crime—yet the state focus of criminal justice systems is overwhelmingly, virtually exclusively, on low level street crimes.

Anarchists also recognize that ruling groups and their stating will *always* define radical and revolutionary activities of the exploited and oppressed as criminal and use the violence of the state to stamp them out. This has been exemplified over the history of often lethal state violence and repression against anarchists. It is, of course, the history of settler colonial state violence against Indigenous resistance and racist state violence against Black resistance movements in the United States from slave revolts to #BlackLivesMatter.

Anarchists view the state as an illegitimate arbitrators of right and wrong, good and bad, acceptable and unacceptable in society. The state is always an interested player. It is never neutral. And throughout the history of capitalism it has acted against movements of the working class, exploited and oppressed, in favor of capital.

Yet some would argue that political prisoners have become separated from resistance movements today, in a period where the prison industrial complex has grown and neoliberal punitive accumulation has spread socially. This separation is partly an outcome of state imprisonment practices that move prisoners away from the locales in which they organized and in which their immediate comrades still reside. It is partly an outcome of specific practices of separation including restrictions on communication for prisoners, etc. As well prisoners are faced with the day to day realities of survival within jails and prisons.

Current efforts can draw on long and rich histories of anarchist attacks against prisons and prison systems. The Revolutionary Insurrection Army in Ukraine, often referred to as Makhnovists in regard to their prominent anarchist organizer Nestor Makhno, blew up police stations and released prisoners in areas they liberated during the Russian Revolution and Civil War. The volunteer force had to fight off assaults from both bourgeois (White) armies and Bolshevik (Red) armies. The anarchist militia, the Iron Column, active during the Spanish Revolution and Civil War in the 1936 period, were known to have liberated prisoners from San Miguel de los Reyes prison. Liberated prisoners often joined the Iron Column in its battles against fascist forces.

## 1    Prisoner Support

There has grown over the last several decades a real disjuncture between working class communities and movements and political prisoners. Even activists have largely lost touch with those comrades imprisoned for organizing only a generation or two before.

That situation is recently changing, perhaps in fundamental ways. As the state clampdown on alternative globalization activists and organizers grows, and as community organizers face jail time under extreme charges such as conspiracy, it is inevitable that more people from contemporary movements will find themselves inside prisons as political prisoners—or will be required to support comrades who have been taken inside.

During the period from the 1980s up to the first decades of the twenty-first century, the lessons, experiences, words, and guidance of political prisoners were kept alive by the efforts of a few dedicated people and groups, such as the Anarchist Black Cross, the anarchist producers of the "Certain Days" political prisoners support calendar, and the publisher of armed struggle literature Kersplebedeb.

At this point in time, with increasingly repressive criminal justice policies and practices there are clearly obstacles to collaboration between prisoners and outsiders in the growing resistance to global capital. Yet, this repression will bring new activists into the prisons and open opportunities for overcoming some of the physical barriers to interaction.

More and more the politically mobilized will be compelled to engage with and learn from those members of our movements who have been imprisoned. Thankfully there are works like *Defying the Tomb* that insurgents can turn to for analysis and information.

Activists like Kevin Rashid Johnson came to recognize that the conditions in prison—indeed the very existence of prisons—could not be changed without fundamental changes in socioeconomic conditions—the broader social structures of capitalism. He went from reformer to abolitionist—a move from a critical to a radical criminological perspective.

The struggle for political prisoners, and against prisons, is also an anticapitalist struggle. It is necessary that we recognize the unity of the struggle against racist oppression and the class struggle for socialist revolution (and the place of criminal justice systems within these struggles).

Prisons have been an essential tool in state capitalist capacity to manufacture discontinuity in popular struggles. Imprisonment has broken the link between struggles of the 1960s and 1970s and today. At the same time this discontinuity has allowed for the expansion and consolidation of state capitalist rule (Johnson, 290). This weapon has been deployed especially against Black people and Indigenous people in the US and Canada respectively. It has made prisoners of political activists and organizers.

For Johnson, "mass involvement or sympathy with organized tactical armed resistance is the one form of struggle that truly endangers empire's power" (293). Infrastructures of resistance provide a logistical base for building mass support. Many of these infrastructures were destroyed and/or demobilized following the state repression against the upsurge of the late 1960s and early 1970s. The "war on crime" played a part in this.

There will be dedicated efforts by states and capital to isolate the armed front from the masses. In the 1960s and 1970s, Daniel Patrick Moynihan advised the Nixon administration to achieve this goal partly by criminalizing the image of the armed front. As today, revolutionary activity became constructed as terrorism. Concerted efforts were also put into dissolving the lower strata grassroots support and replacing it with middle class social conformity and moralism.

The "war on crime" initiated first under Nixon, was directed at stopping the spread of organized armed resistance and the militant tactics of working class and poor youth, particularly Black youth. Under NSC 46 the government explicitly stated that continued growth of Black struggles for economic justice in the 1970s would require violent repression from the government to stabilize the social relations of working class and poor communities. NSC 46 noted that such steps would be "misunderstood" both inside and outside the US and could lead to further trouble for the administration (314).

Middle strata elites, with interests in access to and maintenance of capitalist markets, undermine and eventually replace working class and poor people among the grassroots leadership. Revolutionary activities and armed struggle tactics are demonized and degraded. Existing institutions are presented as means for meeting social needs and energies are channeled toward statist or market based institutions and practices. As Johnson notes:

> The ensuing mass incarceration, criminalization, concentration of police and surveillance, and the vast Prison-Industrial Complex targeted especially at poor, urban Blacks, has been a conscious tactical response of empire to repress anti-colonial, anti-capitalist, and revolutionary fervor amongst the oppressed classes. (298–299)

The lie of government claims about social welfare costs is readily revealed in prison expansion. As Johnson puts it:

> the irony being that as we languish, forgotten and with minds rotting, inside these steel and concrete humyn warehouses, the government will provide us freely with the very necessities, (food, clothing, shelter, medical care), that it denies us out in society; the denial of which drove most of us to "crime" in the first place. (344)

As Tom Big Warrior suggests in the "Afterword": "They were fighting back before they knew what they were up against" (373).

Ironically, perhaps, it was only in prison that they gained access to the literature that would help them properly understand their experiences. This revolutionary theory was itself brought into prison environments as a result of the mass incarcerations of political prisoners in the 1960s and 1970s, including members of the Black Panther Party, American Indian Movement, and Black Liberation Army.

It is a reflection on social conditions that prisons have been sites of revolutionary upsurge in the neoliberal period. Prison populations have expanded exponentially over the last 30 years as incarceration has replaced social housing and other programs that addressed, if inadequately, pressing social issues like poverty. This is a class war and there are many POWs.

## 2    The Anarchist Black Cross

The Anarchist Black Cross is perhaps the most prominent prisoners' support group in the global North and has been at the forefront of struggles for liberty and freedom in solidarity with prisoners over the course of the twentieth and twenty-first centuries. The ABC (and more recent Anarchist Black Cross Federation, ABCF) organizes material and legal resources for political prisoners. It also provides political literature and educational materials for prisoners and for the general public. There are ABCF groups in Austin, Texas, Los Angeles, Pittsburgh, Philadelphia, Denver, New York City, and Toronto, among other locations.

The Anarchist Red Cross was formed following a break from the Political Red Cross (PRC) which was controlled by Social Democrats. The Political Red Cross had been formed to support political prisoners in Czarist Russia. The Social Democrat leadership refused to provide support to anarchist and Social Revolutionary political prisoners in Russia, even as anarchists and Social Revolutionaries contributed donations for political prisoners. The anarchists viewed this as a treason against resistance and organized the ARC to support the anarchist and Social Revolutionary political prisoners excluded by the Social Democrats.

Anarchist writer and theorist Rudolf Rocker, a treasurer for the ARC in London, claimed that the group was founded around the period before the first Russian Revolution of 1905. Exiled revolutionaries formed branches of the group in other areas of the United States and England after the settled as exiles in those locations, especially London, New York, and Chicago.

Another origin story, by founding member Harry Weinstein, says the group was founded in the summer of 1906. Weinstein and others were providing clothes to anarchists sentenced to exile in Siberia. Anarchists were imprisoned in Artvisky Prison, a notorious hard labor prison in Siberia.

Yet another record traces the group's origins to 1907 at the time of two conferences in London, England in July and August of that year. It is said that anarchists and Social Revolutionaries met, under the initiative of Social Revolutionary Vera Figner, to discuss the struggles of political prisoners in Russia. It is suggested that this marks the founding of the international section of the Anarchist Red Cross, after the earlier founding of the London and New York groupings.

With the 1917 Revolution in Russia, anarchists, along with other revolutionaries, believed that a new society was about to take history's stage. So optimistic were they that they disbanded the ARC. Many exiled revolutionaries looked forward to a return home to participate in the revolutionary transformation of society. This would, of course, prove premature as anarchist faced severe repression under the emerging Bolshevik regime. After only a few months of disbandment, the anarchists were compelled to restart the ARC.

Eventually they took on the Black Cross designation to symbolize explicitly the black flag of anarchy. The name change occurred during the Russian Civil War, and was done in part to avoid confusion with the International Red Cross which was also active in Russia. During this period the ABC began organizing self-defense units as well a need that arose given the military assaults against anarchists coming from multiple sides.

Nestor Makhno was involved in organizing chapters of the ABC as a compliment to the Revolutionary Insurrectionary Army of Ukraine. Their activities went beyond prisoner support to provide self-defense and emergency medical services. Under attack from the multiple forces of the Cossacks, White armies, and the Red Army, the Ukrainian Black Cross engaged in city defense efforts and urban militia activities.

Under the Bolsheviks in the early years of the Russian Revolution, ARC aid workers were arrested and incarcerated. In 1919 there were mass arrests of anarchists across Russia. New needs arose to support anarchist prisoners of the Bolsheviks. New groups were formed to support anarchist prisoners but the Bolsheviks criminalized aid workers supporting anarchists under charges that they were "aiding criminal elements" as anarchists were then designated by the new state. Red Guards disrupted and confiscated aid shipments to anarchist prisoners.

ABC stayed active in a variety of formations under different banners over the next several decades. These were still viewed as part of the Anarchist Red Cross/Anarchist Black Cross movements. The ABC was revived actively and explicitly in the 1960s in Britain through the efforts of Stuart Christie and Albert Meltzer, largely to support anarchist prisoners in Francisco Franco's Spain. Christie himself had been jailed in Spain and knew there were no international groups working to support anarchist prisoners in Spain.

During the 1980s ABC groups developed in the United States who became active around a range of prison issues. This growth continued through the 1990s and saw collectives form in Canadian cities like Toronto as well.

In 1995 several chapters in the United States regrouped to form the Anarchist Black Cross Federation (ABCF). Other ABC formations existed in their own networks. The Break the Chains conference held in August of 2003 brought the formations together in closer arrangements for supportive action

Unlike some anarchist groupings, the Anarchist Black Cross Federation does not view all prisoners as political prisoners. They emphasize the more than 100 prisoners in the United States who are imprisoned for their conscious, intentional, political organizing and resistance actions. A political prisoner is viewed as an enemy of the state in comparison with a social prisoner who is imprisoned as part of an unjust system's regular functioning. At the same time it is recognized that many social prisoners will become politicized in prison and then subjected to special punishment and mistreatment.

In the view of the ABCF:

> Though some have a wider definition of Political Prisoners, we maintain that even if the definition of a Political Prisoner was expanded and widely accepted to include social prisoners of conscience, it needs to be clear that those prisoners who went to prison as a result of political action taken on the street would still demand our priority support. For movements to support other prisoners before we support the prisoners who have gone to prison for building the very movements we now participate in is backwards and criminal.
>
> Political Prisoners and Prisoners of War are not in prison for committing social "crimes," nor are they criminals. Different PP/POWs participated in progressive and revolutionary movements in varying levels. Some in educational and community organizing, others in clandestine armed and offensive people's armies. All are in prison as a result of conscious political action, for building resistance, building and leading movements and revolution... for making change.

The ABCF communicates with as many political prisoners and prisoners of war as they are able to. This includes determining types of support and services needed. Among the work done is developing financial support for phone calls and postage stamps so that prisoners can communicate with friends, family, and comrades on the outside. This is key. So too is provision of clothing and footwear. Subscriptions and books are also provided as essential resources.

The federation's Prisoners' Committee (PC) consists of five political prisoners/prisoners of war and they rotate yearly. The Prisoners' Committee's responsibilities include, in part:

1.    Allocating funds of the Warchest Program to PP/POWs.
2.    Allocating Emergency Funds from the Warchest Program.

3.    Voting on policy and proposals of the Federation.
4.    Confirming the legitimacy of prisoners claiming PP/POW status.
5.    Submitting and help develop proposals.
6.    Staying in communication with other FC members

Funds are raised through a Warchest Program. This consists of monthly donations from ABC groups as well as one-time donations. Cheques of $30 are sent
out monthly to prisoners. ABCF organizes a run, Running Down the Walls, in
prison and in the streets as a fundraiser. The annual run occurs in cities including New York, Los Angeles, and Denver.

Informational materials are also produced. This includes recording tapes,
shirts, calendars, fliers, booklets, and pamphlets. These provide information
about prisoners, their struggles and the movements that they are part of.

The ABCF also works to keep political prisoners connected with the movements and communities they were involved in prior to criminalization. This
part of the work of keeping people connected and healthy but also building
movements. It recognizes that all who do resistance work can and will be targeted and the state cannot be allowed to determine the history and trajectory
of people's involvement in their movements.

The ABCF explains the situation of political prisoners and the pressing demands of the work as follows:

> As enemies of the state, they serve the hardest time. The government of-
> ten attempts to lock them far away from their families, friends and sup-
> porters. We must not allow them to be isolated. When geographically
> possible, we go into the prisons and visit PP/POWs. This also brings the
> harsh reality of political imprisonment much closer to supporters. It re-
> minds us that PP/POWs are not only names and figures, pictures on our
> T-shirts and leaflets, but people with personalities and personal needs.
> And if we forget this or neglect to include it in our work to defend them,
> our foundations will soon become weak.

Anarchists must be active for comrades on the inside who are still part of and
making significant contributions to resistance movements.

## 3    The General Defense Committee

The General Defense Committee (GDC) of the Industrial Workers of the World
(IWW) seeks to support and defend all members of the working class who are
subjected to state persecution, repression, and violence for their activities related to class struggle. This is borne of a recognition, through vast experience,

that organizers are and will be targeted by the state and capital or their activities in advancing working class interests and revolutionary aims of the exploited and oppressed. Without concerted and coordinated defense efforts, and infrastructures and resources, organizers can be isolated and separated from communities and workplaces and resistance broken.

A member of the IWW or GDC who is in good standing can petition the General Defense Committee for aid in legal defense against charges related to actions, including strikes and political actions, protests, pickets, etc. Support might include legal aid, bail, court fees, etc. Assistance can be in the form of grants or interest free loans. Support also includes public education about a case, letter writing campaigns in support of someone who is criminalized and in a call for the dropping of charges, and so on.

The IWW and the GDC also extend solidarity to non-members of either group who are targeted by the state for political repression and processing through the criminal justice system. They provide support in the form of motions of public support, letter writing campaigns, and public education in relation to the specific case (or cases) involved. In practice, IWW and GDC members offer on the ground support for non-members who are targeted by the state for political repression, where there is an IWW and/or GDC present locally.

In their 2017 Referendum, the General Defense Committee passed a Preamble to their bylaws. It reads as follows:

### Preamble

The capitalist class of bosses, financiers, landlords, and their cops wage relentless and violent class war upon the working class. The General Defense Committee (GDC) is a committee of and supports the revolutionary unionism of the Industrial Workers of the World (IWW). The GDC's goal is to defend and support the entire working class, divided and under attack by those who wage class war against us. We therefore promote, through organization, action, and outreach, a mass, non-sectarian defense of the class, in order to build a self-organized working class that treats differences as strengths and opportunities to live in solidarity. Community Self Defense means we intend to build our revolutionary community precisely by defending it and the earth on which we live.

Our power as a class will never come from our possession of wealth, but from our ability to organize the class to defend ourselves. We must secure defense against legal attacks, but do not imagine that legal and financial defense alone are sufficient. Any revolutionary union that does not expect oppression from the master class, and organize to meet it, has failed to learn from past waves of repression.

We say defense means organized action taken explicitly to defend members of the class against the different forms of oppression that structure our society. Our membership expects the GDC to be an arena of mutual education through mutual struggle. Exploiters rely upon the fractured unity of the working class. By standing in solidarity across and directly attacking the diverse oppressions of the class, we intend to embody the notion that an injury to one really is an injury to all, and to openly use our defense to build the resilience, strength, and fighting spirit of the working class. Because the class war is not limited to the workplace, our defense of the class cannot be limited to the workplace. Oppressions like racism and sexism structure class oppression and division. Both degrade the solidarity members of the working class should have for each other, and are predicated on acts of violence within the class, and structures of violence organized by the state. We are against all oppressions. By organizing against the diverse oppressions of the working class, and centering our revolutionary and anti-capitalist foundations, we intend to directly overcome those divisions. Through this struggle we advance the goal of an anti-capitalist revolution by building the size, solidarity, and strength of working class.

The oppressed do not determine the grounds of their liberation; those grounds are chosen by the oppressors, whose warfare upon our class results in exclusion, harm, and death. We intend to meet our oppressors on whatever grounds we must, in order to complete the revolution against the capitalism that accelerates not only our exploitation throughout the world, but our entire world's ecological peril. We reject sterile bureaucratic or legalistic restrictions on the revolutionary demands with which our union and our world is faced, recognizing that our history includes failed attempts to pretend allegiance to the state and capitalism. We make no pretense. We will defend and support each other.

The General Defense Committee of the Industrial Workers of the World demands hope and bravery of its membership, so that we can build and organize the class that is worthy of the revolution that we must make.

The General Defense Committee is also expanding its vision in the context of rising far right movements and neo-fascist formations. In specific locales like Vancouver there have been active discussions about developing the GDC as a community defense nucleus. This would work to defend people and communities from attack by violent right forces as well as the legal defense requirements that arise after clashes between antifascist and fascist forces on the streets, when police typically target antifascists for violence and criminalization. All of this is part of integrated class struggles.

## 4      The Incarcerated Workers Organizing Committee

Organizing among prisoners, and in support of prisoners has long been part of the work of the Industrial Workers of the World, and other syndicalist groups. The Industrial Workers of the World also support a prisoner led section, the Incarcerated Workers Organizing Committee (iwoc). The iwoc is organized toward the abolition of prison slavery, and prisons more broadly in campaigns supported by allies on the outside. They have branches in more than 15 prisons in the United States which are very active under the most vicious of conditions for organizing. Membership is free to prisoners and supporters are asked to support prisoners with dues of five dollars per month.

The iwoc describes the situation of prison exploitation as follows:

> Incarcerated people are legally slaves as per the 13th Amendment which abolished "slavery and involuntary servitude, except as punishment for a crime" We are legally slaves. If you've been to prison you'd know we are treated like slaves.
>
> Billions are made annually off our backs. Outrageously priced or grossly inadequate privatized "services" like health care, food, phone calls, assault our humanity—they feed us like animals, suck our families dry, and when sick leave us to die. The government spends as much as an elite college tuition per person to keep each of us incarcerated, but this money does not develop us as human beings, reduce crime or make our communities safer.
>
> They also profit from our labor. At least half of the nation's 1.5 million of us imprisoned in the United States have jobs yet are paid pennies an hour, or even nothing at all. Many of us perform the essential work needed to run the prisons themselves—mopping cellblock floors, preparing and serving food, filing papers and other prison duties. Others of us work in "correction industries" programs performing work in areas such as clothing and textile, computer aided design, electronics, and recycling activities. Some of us even sub-contract with private corporations such as Sprint, Starbucks, Victoria's Secret, and many more.
>
> As incarcerated workers, we are some of the most exploited workers in the country. There is no minimum wage for prison labor. The average

wage is 20 cents an hour, with some states not paying a wage at all. Up to 80% of wages can be withheld by prison officials. There are very few safety regulations and no worker's compensation for injury on the job. While in prison, we try to earn money to support our families, ourselves, and pay victim restitution yet these wages prevent us from that. We believe that as workers we are guaranteed the same protections and wages as other workers.

We are working to abolish prison slavery and this system that does not correct anyone or make communities safer.

The IWOC published a Statement of Purpose of July 31, 2014. It reads as follows:

1.  To further the revolutionary goals of incarcerated people and the IWW through mutual organizing of a worldwide union for emancipation from the prison system.
2.  To build class solidarity amongst members of the working class by connecting the struggle of people in prison, jails, and immigrant and juvenile detention centers to workers struggles locally and worldwide.
3.  To strategically and tactically support prisoners locally and worldwide, incorporating an analysis of white supremacy, patriarchy, prison culture, and capitalism.
4.  To actively struggle to end the criminalization, exploitation, and enslavement of working class people, which disproportionately targets people of color, immigrants, people with low income, LGBTQ people, young people, dissidents, and those with mental illness.
5.  To amplify the voices of working class people in prison, especially those engaging in collective action or who put their own lives at risk to improve the conditions of all.

The IWOC has become among the most active and vital sectors of the IWW. It poses a model for solidarity and militant action in specific circumstances of extreme repression. It also highlights necessary, and increasingly important, struggles within the context of crisis state capitalism (see Shantz 2016).

## 5     Prison Strike

September 9, 2016 saw the start of what was the largest prison strike in US history. Anarchists helped to build some of the infrastructure for the strike, working more than a year ahead of the action to prepare the ground for action. This work built upon years of prisoner support and solidarity work that anarchists have been involved in building relationships of trust and support. Anarchist connections have included prison visits, books to prisoners programs, solidarity campaigns, publicity work, etc.

Anarchists have produced numerous zines and other publications supporting prisoners and condemning systems of the prison-industrial-complex. They have organized conferences and public events to discuss the issues and promote strike actions.

In Bloomington, Indiana, anarchists organized assemblies to plan actions in solidarity with the prison strike. These were large organizing meetings but innovated beyond the agreement models of assemblies like Occupy where whole group consensus prevailed. These assemblies eschewed the "tyranny of the majority" to provide spaces where anyone could bring forward proposals for an action. If anyone wanted to take part in a proposed activity they could simply get together and collaborate to do so. Broader discussions would address the proposals but there was no decision making authority apart from or above those who agreed to take on responsibility and organize and carry out actions. This was done as a conscious rejection of (and lesson learned from) the often defeatist and dampening bottleneck of Occupy processes where everything required a General Assembly consensus. This ended up, in practice, instituting what some view as a tedious bureaucracy. For the Bloomington anarchists, this is nothing more than a populist absurdity. Assemblies in Bloomington were robust and held daily.

I might point out that our collective took this non-bureaucratic and participatory approach to decisions and actions a decade before Occupy in the Anarchist Free Space. And it works to some effect. Anyone agreeing to work on an action could do so without complete assent of the group. If people did not want to take part they did not need to. But they could not block those who did. There were, to be sure, discussions around public descriptions of the actions, explanatory statements, and accountability (so those acting were not claiming to be acting on behalf of non-participants as a group or framing actions in politically irresponsible ways).

6     Broad Movement Support

Anarchists have developed agile support systems for activists arrested during protests and other actions or targeted for community organizing activities. Immediately this involves jail support for people who are arrested. This involves arranging lawyers and people to serve as sureties to provide bail. It also involves showing up at court to show support openly and visibly. In cases of mass

arrests in can include noise demonstrations of dozens of people or more outside jails and police stations to let prisoners know that they are not alone and
the movement stands with them. They are in there for us and we are out here
for them.

On an essential level there are the aspects of court support. It is crucial to
show up in court in decent numbers to show that people are supported and to
help them with friendly faces ad shows of solidarity in times of stress for prisoners. At the same time it is crucial to show the courts and public that these are
valued community members who are part of broader social contexts and relationships and social concerns.

On another level is the day-to-day organizing of legal defense teams. This
often includes working with lawyers to provide formal defenses for people. In
many contexts activist lawyers are involved in movements specifically to provide legal supports and defense. There is much organizing work to ensure that
lawyers understand movement issues, perspectives, and commitments beyond
legal formality and feasibility. Or the political arguments against taking the
easiest legal route or action.

Anarchist Black Cross and other prison solidarity organizers hold noise rallies outside prisons to let prisoners know that broader groups of people on the
outside know about them and support them. Big noise rallies are held outside
prisons across the United States to ring in the new year on New Year's Eve.
These take New Year's Eve celebrations to people who cannot celebrate and to
give them a sense of solidarity in a context in which society is socialized to
forget or ignore prisoners. This is perhaps a small gesture but it is done by
groups that are also involved in day-to-day ongoing organizing with prisoners
throughout the year.

Anarchists at many free spaces and infoshops organize books to prisoners
programs to get reading materials inside to prisoners. This is a matter of basic
solidarity—providing otherwise inaccessible reading materials to people who
need them. There is also a pedagogical aspect in providing useful analysis of
social institutions and processes of exploitation, oppression, and repression to
people who are teaching themselves and seeking to gain more knowledge
about the systems and processes that are exploiting and oppressing, and repressing them. In addition there is the need for knowledge about specific legal
information for defending themselves.

Books to prisoners projects involve connecting with prisoners and getting
addresses to send books. Collection boxes are typically set up in free spaces and
infoshops so people can drop off books to send. Specific requests can be made
based on prisoners' interests. Often times people will buy books at the spaces
or infoshops specifically to send to prisoners. Anarchists will bring books in

after they have read them to pass along to prisoners. Usually meetings are organized (weekly, biweekly, monthly) to package the books and get them ready to be mailed. In some cases prisoners have gotten involved in anarchist spaces after release through connections made in books to prisoners programs.

Organizing basics for prisoner support can include organizing car rides on regular schedules to get visitors to prisons to visit prisoners. Other work can include fund raising to get money into prisoners' canteen funds to allow for purchases of necessities inside. Work is also done to support court dates and appearances.

Beyond that there is also much work done on specific public campaigns to raise awareness about specific prisoners and the political nature of their cases. Campaigns can also be run to get letters to prisoners. On occasion interviews are arranged with specific prisoners on political issues.

## 7       Against Isolation

Processing by and through the criminal justice system is a horribly traumatic and typically isolating experience. It is literally you alone against the state. Separated from friends, family, and comrades and thrown into a hostile, anonymous , total institution designed specifically to break you down as a unique, holistic, complex, human being—its only purpose.

Prisoner support can be essential to keep people connected to their communities and to offset (if never really overcome) the isolation and loneliness. Even having friendly faces in the seats during court appearances can make a difference.

There have indeed been a number of high profile suicides by activists facing trial or imprisoned in the United States. This includes people whose cases were receiving some national and international attention. The situation of Jeremy Hammond is a sad and telling one.

This is all a reflection of the awfully isolating, despairing, and torturous nature of prisons and imprisonment. It is inherently crushing and brutal, making optimism a real struggle for anyone.

## 8       Criminal Justice and Class Struggle

Support for prisoners makes clear that the basis of criminal justice systems in state capitalist contexts is class based. Class struggle anarchism must involve class wide organizing and social defense. That means maintaining connections with people who are criminalized. Most of those who are criminalized in liberal democracies are working class and poor people and are most often criminalized for survival strategies, "crimes" of need, etc. Anarchists stress that criminal justice systems are devised and deployed to reinforce and maintain systems of economic inequality and exploitation for the accumulation and preservation of capital and for defense of systems of private ownership and control of social resources. Supporting prisoners is an acknowledgement of these systems and the profound need to develop class solidarity to dismantle them.

Prisoner solidarity work has also contributed to cracking the stigma and social degradation of prisoners by media and criminal justice systems alike. It helps to overcome the demonization of prisoners. At the same time it is part of educating the public about the unjust nature of criminal justice systems in state capitalist political economies.

Fundamentally anarchists are abolitionists and would get rid of criminal justice and prison systems. They would see the end of systems that segregate people on the basis of criminalization and unequal application of class based laws and punitive practices.

## 9       Conclusion

It is a fact of life for anti-statist activists that they will be targeted by the state for repression. This has, of course, been true throughout the history of anarchism. So it is the case that many anarchists will be made prisoners of the state. It also means that maintaining anarchist forces means maintaining connections with comrades who have been targeted and captured by the state. In the present context of the military-industrial-complex there is important organizing work to be done inside prisons as well. Recently anarchists have worked to support prisoner labor organizing and strikes against prison industries and conditions of labor exploitation within prisons. This includes material support as well as ideas and awareness raising about the strikes and prisoner activism among people on the outside.

# CHAPTER 10

# Anarchists against (and within) the Edu-Factory: The Critical Criminology Working Group

This chapter offers a critical analysis of organizing efforts to develop an anarchist working group that is fighting marketization, "job ready" curricula and programs/degrees, and administrative inaccessibility in a new university (converted from a community college) structured within a two-tier post-secondary model (one favoring research schools and supplemented by "teaching" oriented "special purpose" universities geared towards the labor market) by a neoliberal government (in British Columbia). It examines anarchist pedagogical approaches in practice, through organizing, engagement, and struggle.

The Critical Criminology Working Group (CCWG) at Kwantlen Polytechnic University (KPU) in Surrey, British Columbia (Metro Vancouver, unceded Coast Salish territory) is a collective of faculty, students, and community members who organize public events, engage in community organizing, and maintain public media venues. They are now in their fourth year of organizing successful events under difficult circumstances. The Critical Criminology Working Group organizes and hosts a variety of substantial public discussions, including panel discussions, book launches, film screenings, spoken word, and mixed media presentations. It has also organized community actions, including a blockade against a highway through a residential area. The objective has been the engagement of academic work and analysis with issues of broader community concern and the development of participatory, critical pedagogical praxis. It is applied theory in the service of a public criminology bringing together community members, students, and faculty for conversation and action.

Events are an active expression of applied critical knowledge presenting a participatory, open, engaged version of a polytechnic mandate to bring academic work to bear on understanding public issues and contributing to community-based approach to addressing social questions. This is counter to the notion of polytechnic education as job training asserted by administration and the government.

All events have involved participation from community members, students, and faculty, bridging the gap between campus and community. The working group has built alliances with community organizers as well as creating spaces/practices on campus to pose critical pedagogical practices and perspectives. The working group has opposed, within the context of a criminology department, the construction of students as future criminal justice systems workers (and along the way produced some anarchist scholarship and a thesis within and against that structural framework). The chapter also analyses neoliberalism and corporatization within the new universities in British Columbia.

## 1    Anarchism and Criminology

Criminology is often viewed, with some justification, as a conservative, even reactionary discipline. This is due to the association among some faculty with criminal justice system institutions as well as the role, historically and currently, of criminology and, especially, criminal justice programs in recruiting and training future police officers, prison guards, lawyers, and security personnel. It also relates to the tendency of too many criminology scholars to take the statist criminal justice system for granted as a legitimate and proper (even beneficial) institutional framework for defining, addressing, and/or solving social problems.

At the same time there have been important critical, indeed radical, traditions within criminology. And these have often drawn explicitly from anarchism. Indeed anarchism provided some of the earliest criminological theories and offered some of the first opposition to conservative and statist criminology (as represented in the works of Lombroso, for example).

Yet these histories are often forgotten or overlooked within criminology itself, never mind outside the discipline. Thus some are surprised to hear of an anarchist grouping of criminology faculty and students active around a range of social issues in a suburban area out of the activist spotlight.

For the Working Group members, if criminology is to be at all meaningful in addressing social harms, the theoretical and scholarly research tools of criminology can best be used to identify, understand, explain, and respond to the real sources of most social harms—economic and political powerholders and institutions of economic and political power, states and capital.

The Critical Criminology Working Group has attempted to bring anarchist principles, politics, and pedagogies to bear on social struggles in an area otherwise lacking in activist resources. Along the way it has provided growing infrastructures for community organizing while also shifting perceptions of the discipline and challenging the conventional labor market focus of the postsecondary institution in which it is situated.

Students have additionally undertaken innovative research to uncover and resituate anarchist approaches within ongoing practices of criminology, from the early days of the discipline through to the present. They have also carried out original research on corporate and state crime and injustices within dominant criminal justice systems and institutions (and relationships of these with KPU administration).

## 2    The Critical Criminology Working Group

The Critical Criminology Working Group is a collective of Kwantlen faculty, students, and community members who organize public speaking events and a public criminology website. They are now in their fourth year of organizing successful events. The Critical Criminology Working Group organizes and hosts a variety of substantial public discussions, including panel discussions, book launches, film screenings, spoken word, and mixed media presentations. These typically take place over two to three hours. The objective is the engagement of academic work and analysis with issues of broader community concern. It is applied theory in the service of a public criminology, and critical activist pedagogy, bringing together community members, students, and faculty for conversation.

All Critical Criminology Working Group events have been and will continue to be open to faculty, students, and the general public. There has been regular attendance from community members from Langley, Richmond, Surrey, and Vancouver. In addition we have had visitors from Central and South America, several states in the US, and Quebec. Attendees have been a range of ages and backgrounds. Critical Criminology Working Group events have been attended by between 30 to 100 people with the average attendance around 60 people.

Working Group events are an active expression of applied critical knowledge, in keeping with a polytechnic mandate to bring academic work to bear on understanding public issues and contributing to community-based approach to addressing social questions. All events have involved participation from community members, students, and faculty, bridging the gap between campus and community.

KPU students are overwhelmingly from blue collar backgrounds and live in a lower income suburb of Metro Vancouver. A large proportion are from migrant backgrounds and most are the first generation in the family to attend post-secondary education. They have a gut level sense of being exploited and oppressed but often lack means to articulate their frustration or anger. Students benefit greatly by having opportunities for rich and lively discussions of issues of public relevance as developed through the Working Group. They are introduced to speakers and ideas that they might not otherwise have access to. This expands their own personal awareness and understanding while also introducing them to practical solutions by which people and communities are attempting to address these issues. Students have gained access to materials (research reports, pamphlets, books) that have been useful for class projects and term papers. Students have made it clear that participation in Working Group events has opened them up to perspectives and social situations that they would otherwise not have been aware of. Events have made a real contribution to the development of an intellectual culture at Kwantlen in which learning takes place outside the classroom as well as inside.

Faculty members have gained by building research and pedagogical relationships with community members and international scholars. Connections have been made between Kwantlen faculty and community groups in Surrey. This has in turn contributed to opportunities for community-based learning for students. It has also helped with the groundwork for other projects such as the proposed Centre for Social Justice which faculty members in Criminology and Sociology have been busy working towards. Ongoing projects, such as the Climate Teach-Ins about local road and pipeline developments, which involve community members of diverse backgrounds have been initiated through Working Group events.

Events have had participation from recognized academics as well as public intellectuals allowing for the cross-pollination of ideas that characterizes polytechnic education. Participants consistently report that the events have raised their awareness of Kwantlen and left them with a highly favorable view of the University. Indeed, past out of town presenters (including Yves Engler and Test) have contacted the Working Group to host other events in Surrey. They now include Kwantlen as a potential site for a visit during national tours, a development that has only resulted from the efforts of the Working Group. These are public figures with high profiles of their own who bring many people to Kwantlen who otherwise have not had occasion to attend the campus.

Kwantlen has benefited from increased positive exposure and notice within a range of local and international media. Kwantlen has also benefited from increased connections and strengthened relations with the communities in which we work and which we serve. There has also been a benefit by providing students with enriched learning experiences beyond the classroom. In keeping with Kwantlen's polytechnic mandate Working Group events involve a productive intersection of theory and practice.

The Working Group also maintains a website and mailing list with news postings and notices of their events. In addition they produce the journal *Radical Criminology* (now in production on the fourth issue). The CCWG also has an active website and a Twitter account with more than 5800 followers. They have also established a YouTube channel and publish videos from some of their events (http://www.youtube.com/user/RadicalCriminology). They have published the video from the September 17 2013 event on Palestinian Political Prisoners as well as the October 8 2013 presentation by Layla AbdelRahim on "Crime and Reward from an Anarcho-Primitivist Perspective." The November 26, 2013 event on "Human Rights and Community Advocacy in the Age of Extreme Energy" was recorded by a community videographer and is also presented on YouTube (http://www.youtube.com/watch?v=88zE_cElbxw). Working Group events have also generated media attention. The "Scrap the So-Called 'Terror List!'" event was featured in the *Georgia Straight* (with notice on the cover).

The Working Group has also given rise to related longer term projects including the Kwantlen Center for Anarchist Studies (KCAS). A new, still evolving, project, KCAS will provide digital online copies of rare movement documents as well as providing library space for hard copy originals. The KCAS will eventually provide research support for activists and scholars interested in anarchist movements. Some of the documents made available at KCAS represent the sole remaining copies of the publication. This includes numerous Xeroxed zines and pamphlets that were produced in relatively small numbers.

Additionally, the Working Group also produces an original journal of radical theory and practice that brings together academics and community and prison activists. The journal, *Radical Criminology*, is now into its sixth issue since launching in 2012.

The CCWG also hosted the North American Anarchist Studies Network Fifth Annual Conference. Over the past two decades, there's been a growing interest, both inside and outside the academy, in research done on anarchism (or by anarchists), and we have seen a resurgence in related multidisciplinary reading, study and theory. As the conference call suggested:

> It is hoped that this conference will build upon the work of the four successful previous NAASN conferences; first, as a wonderful opportunity for head-to-head gathering, with lively discussion and comradely debate, and then at conclusion, will leave an open archive of all published papers & presentations intended to stand as a positive contribution to the further flourishing of anarchist ideas and action.

As part of the conference the CCWG organized the first ever anarchist bookfair in Surrey. This was a considerable move for organizing in the area. Indeed, many local activists upon hearing that an anarchist bookfair was being organized in Surrey expressed disbelief. "Seriously, an anarchist bookfair *in Surrey*?!?" was a common response. The general disdain with which Surrey has been held among activists is discussed in greater detail below. Yet the bookfair and conference were major successes, bring more than 500 people to Surrey for several lively days of engaged discussion, debate, music, art, and revelry. Several participants proclaimed it the best anarchist bookfair they had attended, more engaging than several loner standing, larger fairs. Requests are already being made for tables at next year's (2015) event.

KPU is also, as a former community college, a commuter school without student residences and lacking even a student center as spaces where students might congregate and interact. Part of the culture at the school has been that students go to class and then go home without lingering. The Working Group has worked, with success, to change this culture. People now organize their schedules around working group events. While the first few meetings were sparsely attended (a dispiriting experience that has caused other groups to give up hosting events) the Working Group has committed to put on events on a regular basis and to follow through with compelling presentations and discussions regardless of attendance. Over time there has grown a recognition that if the Working Group hosts an event it will be lively, engaging, interesting, and meaningful.

## 3      Structures of Collaboration

As is true for most anarchist collectives, the Working Group operates according to a horizontal organizational approach. There are no designated positions such as director or convener. All members discuss plans for events and take an open approach to events (avoiding sectarianism) and shared labor in organizing. As an anarchist organization the Working Group favors participatory, egalitarian, flat (or multi-directional) organizing practices.

The Working Group is organized on an affinity group basis. Rather than a formal, unified, membership, it brings together a core of people with shared interests and perspectives—social affinity—and some level of trust. The Working Group consists of a core of organizers who plan, and organize events, do outreach, and organize solidarity actions with community groups around specific campaigns. The core is made up of faculty, students, and community members, who have a shared (informal) basis of agreement around specific issues and perspectives (anti-statism and anti-capitalism). Membership, while informal, is not open to all initially but new members can become part of the organizing core after some time involved with Working Group events and when there is affinity between themselves and group members (on a political rather than personal basis). These are relationships based on mutual respect and trust.

Beyond the organizational core, there are participants, of all types, who support the group and help with events but who do not want to be involved in organizing. Events are open to all.

The affinity group approach for the organizational core, with an open approach in solidarity alliances, has been taken to provide some insulation against uncritical tendencies among criminology faculty—to keep a radical and activist orientation and commitment in a discipline in which both have been marginalized. Indeed some liberal faculty, who are not particularly committed to activism, community organizing, or critical perspectives have sought to join the group and to water down its principles. They are, of course welcomed at meetings where they are invited to engage with the debates and discussions. At the same time the dual approach allows for members to maintain critical support in alliances with non-anarchist groups. Thus a comradely and collegial anarchist perspective can be offered in alliances without hiding or watering down the anarchist orientation in strategy and tactic.

This dual approach allows for development of what some anarchist communists refer to as theoretical and tactical unity. Rather than cobbling together a mish mash of contradictory or opposing perspectives, in a false or limited consensus, and diluting the commitment to libertarian pedagogy and action, the Working Group approach favors strong internal debate to develop more critical analysis and action. This does not mean that sameness or complete agreement is sought but rather that some agreement is had around key issues *after* and *through* discussion and analysis. And the context is always active involvement in real world struggles.

In practice the group has been very open to supporting groups that have different opinions and perspectives and in public events seeks lively engagement over pressing issues, as a means to develop more critical, or radical (getting to the root of social challenges), approaches.

Experiential learning is also valued and tasks are rotated and shared where possible. Skill sharing is a means to facilitate a spread of capabilities and skills, rather than keeping a strict separation of skills among members.

4      SurreyWhat!?!: Anarchy in the Suburban Hinterland

Anarchism is North America has largely been viewed as an urban, indeed downtown phenomenon. Very little attention has been given to, and very little written about, suburban anarchist projects, apart from a few zines and blogs produced by suburban anarchists themselves. There have been very few discussions of the particular issues facing suburban anarchists.

In addition to the political economic context of the polytechnic university under neoliberal marketization attention must be given to the suburban context in which the CCWG organizes. There are the specific challenges posed by the socio-political context of organizing in a blue collar multi-ethnic suburb, far away (culturally and politically as well as spatially) from the activist hubs of downtown Vancouver. The CCWG has worked to overcome these obstacles and provide a useful pedagogical and resistance infrastructure.

Surrey is a too much reviled working class suburb of Metro Vancouver. A shadow city. Not economically peripheral, it is an epicenter of capitalist mega-projects and strip malls, a sprawling convergence of seven superhighways and a massive port expansion.

With multiple rail lines and pipelines already, it's not enough for their greed; the vulture developers are now running in overdrive mode: politicians in pocket, and ready to roll out twice as many more lines. They're pressing hard now in order to facilitate the extraction and shipping of megatons more dirty coal— dug up in Montana and Wisconsin, shipped via rail lines through Washington out to port here and then sold and burned across Pacific to return as acid rain. A battle over LNG expansion and fracking is heating up. Also over heavy fossil fuel transport and leaks. Major pipeline expansion projects are actively being fought all the way from here to the Alberta Tar Sands, the Fraser River and the Salish Sea tangibly threatened by their refineries and supertanker traffic.

Surrey is a city of migrant settlers. Besides English, it is Punjabi and Mandarin which are the most commonly spoken languages. It is a rapidly growing suburb which became a city itself with sprawling satellite suburbs. Often outside of or marginal to the activist cultures of downtown Vancouver but with its own overlooked, unrecognized, histories of working class radicalism.

It started urbanity as a gas station, really, on what was a gold miner's trail, which was trod onto many thousands of years of Indigenous people's settlements as part of a British colonialist imposition, with 1800s displacements still on-going and unfolding in new gentrification and industrial expansion. There are densely rich middens in the rainforest valleys still left along the southern shore of the Fraser. The year-round warmth of the green, wet valleys provided excellent shelter, and became regular "wintering" villages for so many (thousands?) of years, it's literally some of the oldest known settlements in the world.

The Kwantlen peoples ran all across these territories, and still play a vital role in the interconnection and welcome at any All Nation Gathering. Recently, there has been some preliminary steps towards a Truth and Reconciliation Project aimed at uncovering and beginning to address the horrors of colonial rule in the form of Residential Schools (which were genocidal, language—and children—stealing institutions that ran for too many decades throughout these lands). This area, on the Pacific Ocean, is also Semiahmoo territory (particularly in the south, directly adjacent to the US border). It is—partially ceded, partially hotly contested—Musqueam territory (particularly in North Surrey, which is also now a site of a gentrification push by new condo developments). It is Tsawwassen land (to the west, all along the delta "Where the Fraser River Flows" into the Salish Sea). It is Katzie territory in the east, and up into the mountains. Surrey is unceded territory, contested in multiple layering complex ways.

Surrey is looked down upon by more privileged activists living in activist enclaves in neighborhoods rich in progressive sub/cultural capital (collective cafes, anarchist bookstores, artist studios and galleries, organic food shops, alternative theatres, etc.) and used to more activist influenced (and familiar) environs. In Surrey even reliable meeting spaces, let alone cultural venues for shared experiences and discussions, are absent or unavailable. The CCWG is attempting to use educational venues and practices to organize infrastructures of resistance in a context in which these necessary resources for struggle are largely absent or inaccessible.

The Working Group has also supported lower income groups and groupings without resources in funding external events, providing organizing space, providing promotional materials, providing for a for awareness raising, and getting funding to individuals and groups through university honoraria. These have offered significant redistribution for resources for groups and individuals engaged in social struggles. In an area in which durable, reliable, shared spaces for organizing and awareness raising and shared experiences and mutual aid are too often lacking, the Working Group has provided an often crucial infrastructure of resistance.

The CCWG has played vital roles in specific campaigns in Surrey. As one example, the CCWG was a main organizing center for a blockade and occupation camp against development of the South Fraser Perimeter Road, a key artery in the government's planned network of free trade/export processing zones in British Columbia. The free trade zones will be spaces in which environmental and labor protections in the province are suspended for multinational corporations that establish themselves in the province. The road itself had a significant impact on local ecosystems and poor neighborhoods which faced evictions. The CCWG provided meeting space, organizational work, website support and material support for the campaign. Even more, CCWG members were active participants in the blockade and especially in providing logistical support (building supplies, food, labor) for the camp, which lasted for several weeks on a site of road development. Working Group members also engaged in door to door information canvasses in neighborhoods along the road route to provide information about the harms associated with the road. Notably, many people who would go on to take part in Occupy Vancouver and campaigns against pipelines in British Columbia got their feet wet with the anti-road camp; thus showing the important developmental part played by such direct action campaigns.

The Working Group was also instrumental in launching a broad campaign against the federal government's terror list. The terror list is a political tool used by the government to criminalize people, particularly migrants, involved in peoples' liberation or community defense groups by labeling such groups as terrorist (even where they have no history of terrorist activity). The campaign researched and publicized the political nature of the list (targeting progressive groups rather than actually terroristic reactionary ones) and building solidarity campaigns for people targeted by the government. This has been significant given the migrant, working class background of many Surrey residents and the fact that groups connected to the migrant communities in Surrey have been listed.

The CCWG has been successful in breaking down some of the barriers to connecting and organizing that have separated not only activists in Surrey but which have separated activists in Surrey from those in Vancouver. Activists in the downtown have reported to CCWG members that the first or only time they travelled to Surrey (only 30 minutes by Skytrain rapid transit) was for Working Group events.

Surrey, like most of British Columbia, is unceded Indigenous territory. Lands were never negotiated through treaties and native communities did not give up title to their lands. This fact has been of significance for the group and it has taken anti-colonialism as a key organizing principle. Many events are opened with a greeting and welcome from a member or members of the Kwantlen First Nation. Events ate opened with an acknowledgement of the land and the first people on whose territories events are held. Numerous events have addressed directly colonialism and resistance to colonialism. Many events have built solidarity with Indigenous communities in various parts of Turtle Island (North America) who are struggling against resource extraction, neo-colonialism, violence against Indigenous people, and legal system injustices.

People have come to see the Working Group as a valuable and necessary resource for organizing in the Fraser Valley and suburban Vancouver. Notably, in the absence of the Working Group there would have been no Surrey organizing (for the anti-terror list campaign) at all or no anarchist or radical organizing (in the case of the Climate Camp against the SFPR) around the issues.

5      "Special Purpose Teaching Universities" and the
       Neoliberal Edu-Factory

The CCWG also operates within a specific post-secondary educational context.
It is one that highlights changes occurring within the post-secondary sectors in
the Canadian state context. The neoliberal austerity framework and the push
to convert universities from institutions of critical engagement to places of industry service (either for jobs training or research geared to commercialization) has shaped Kwantlen's development from a community college, in the
1980s to a university college, a near-university institution with a vocational
emphasis but a new capacity to grant degrees in limited areas, in the 1990s to a
polytechnic university in 2008. KPU was designated a new "special purpose
teaching university" in 2008 along with four other former colleges in British
Columbia. As a polytechnic university among the special purpose new universities, KPU is envisioned by the British Columbia government as an extension
of the industrial regime in the province, as a labor market training site.

The Liberal government's intention in converting former colleges and university colleges into the new universities is expressed directly within the Act
that governs the "special purpose" institutions. The new University Act, created
at the time the new universities were launched in 2008, states that these are
"special purpose teaching universities" and their purpose is to meet the labor
market demands, and the needs of industry, of the specific regions in which
the new universities are located. They are distinctly hybrid institutions retain-
ing trades and technology programs and facilities along with continuing education, university preparation, and university degree programs.

At the same time the "special purpose teaching universities" are granted
fewer rights and opportunities than the established "traditional" universities,
which include the University of British Columbia (UBC), Simon Fraser University (SFU), the University of Victoria, and the University of Northern British
Columbia (UNBC). Their "special purpose" is clearly as labor market driven job
preparatory institutions. This purpose is reflected in the fact that they are denied government funding for research and scholarship. Research is said to be
allowable in the special purpose teaching university's mandate only "so far as
and to the extent that its resources from time to time permit" and then as "applied research and scholarly activities" (read as job related) And this applied
research and scholarly activity is further limited "to support the programs of
the special purpose, teaching university" rather than for the sake of knowledge
production, intellectual inquiry, critical thinking, or curiosity. Furthermore,
while the research universities are global in scope, the special purpose universities are mandated to serve the (labor market) needs are their specific local

school districts, thus reinforcing their role as job training institutes. The Act further states that the new special purpose teaching universities are not permitted to grant Ph.D.s even where institutional capacity and local need might favor it.

Funds can be raised or saved by the institution for the purposes of research and scholarship but this is not granted directly by the government for these purposes. This is itself a distortion of what a university is and what purpose it has. It is fundamentally a two tiered structure of haves and have nots. It has been challenged in various ways by faculty at each of the institutions.

In addition, the two tiered university structure in British Columbia is also reflected in the fact that faculty salaries are legislatively capped at the special purpose teaching universities. Faculty are also denied tenure, although through collective agreements they achieve similar protections.

The neoliberal market focus of the special purpose teaching universities as expressed in the Act is given further form and content in KPU's Aims and Principles and Mission and Mandate Statement. The Mission and Mandate Statement proclaims:

> We value scholarship as a socially relevant obligation and opportunity. We support multiple approaches to research and innovation to address community, industry, and market needs.

The Vision Statement explains its vision of the polytechnic university: "A Polytechnic: We emphasize applied education within the context of broad-based undergraduate learning to prepare our students for successful and rewarding careers." And further: "Kwantlen provides learning opportunities that support professional and personal enrichment by responding to the needs of the workforce and the interests of our broader community."

## 6        Neoliberalism and Criminology

In the present period of political economic austerity, post-secondary institutions like Kwantlen are pressured by governments and businesses alike to provide dual functions. On the one had they serve a function of training the working class to accept increasingly labor market oriented job related tasks (rather than critical thinking) within a market that is dominated by lower skill, perfunctory, service sector roles. At the same time the schools also function to provide a detour from the tightened job market for a proportion of the working class, keeping unemployed youth off of the streets—in a holding pattern that they pay for. For some students they hold the promise of the relative privilege of low level managerial positions in private industry or state agencies, depending on the discipline. Anarchists have long argued that formal schooling involves inculcation into the dominant norms, values, and beliefs of state capitalist society. Students are taught to internalize acceptable behaviors within this context (rather than to develop values and behaviors that oppose it or provide an alternative). Mainstream criminology has been viewed as a discipline particularly suited to this sort of molding of dominant, particularly statist, values and priorities.

One might note in this regard the veritable explosion of criminology programs designed to prepare working class students to be police, prison guards, and border security or private security guards. The neoliberal context has propelled the rise and expansion of criminology and criminal justice programs to service the expanding repressive state institutions. Thus they are prepared to police their fellow working class neighbors. This is particularly poignant in a blue collar suburb with a large South Asian immigrant population like Surrey, where KPU is located. Surrey has been subject to numerous moral panics over crime, especially around racialized gang discourses centered on Indo-Canadian male youth.

Notably, this has accompanied a shift away from critical theory and social movements courses in sociology—the department in which many criminology programs are housed and from which others have emerged. While sociology is typically politically of the Left and activist influenced, criminology is often more Right wing or conservative. While criminology expands sociology recedes in some institutions.

The Working Group fights back against all of this. It uses the tools of criminology to analyze and challenge state institutions and practices in the neoliberal period. This includes research into university relationships with industry and the character of corporate agreements with the institution. Thus students and faculty have undertaken research looking at questionable agreements between KPU and Sodexo for food services on campus and exclusivity agreements such as the agreement that allows for a monopoly of Coca-Cola products on campus. Research uncovered a correspondence between the timing of the Coke exclusivity agreement and the absence of water fountains in a new campus building and the lack of repair on existing fountains in other buildings.

The Working Group also supported a student led campaign against Sodexo. When a student associated with the CCWG tried to distribute leaflets outlining Sodexo's histories of labor abuse, racism, prison contracts, and unhealthy food, he was assailed by campus security taking directions from the Sodexo management to stop him from speaking with other students and distributing the information sheets. That campus security should be taking direction from an outside corporate manager was clearly a troubling situation. In response the CCWG printed thousands of leaflets and began a mass leafleting campaign with information tables on campus. The CCWG also challenged administration to uphold academic freedom for students and call off security, allowing anyone to freely disseminate information on campus. Another group of students from the CCWG started a grassroots, cooperative free food distribution on campus, providing healthy vegetarian food for free each day. Friends for Food was eventually shut down when Sodexo called the health inspector to fine the students and insist on a permit.

These struggles are ongoing. Notably none would have been undertaken or pursued without the active presence of the Critical Criminology Working Group on campus.


## 7      Conclusion: Breaking Free

In addition to providing a needed resource for community organizing, the Working Group has provided a crucial opportunity for undergraduate students to develop a range of skills, both related to their academic interests (research, writing, communicating publicly, etc.) and to their social justice concerns as community members and activists.

It has also served as a space to support students who are questioning their future careers as state agents in training. Several students have changed their perspectives on the police and guards as well as institutions such as courts and prisons through Working Group events, discussions, and actions. Several have changed career paths as a result of involvement with the Working Group and its organizing efforts.

Many students from blue collar backgrounds, who had been told repeatedly that they could not succeed at graduate school or would be wasting their time and should focus on a job, have developed and successfully pursued their interests in grad school and/or gone on to study to become teachers. This is something of a direct material outcome of Working Group organizing. It has some ideological as well as real world consequence in diverting a potential recruit away from a repressive state agency (police, border services, security, prison guard, etc.) and actually results in their active organizing (with fellow students and beyond) to undermine those agencies.

Even more, students and others involved in the Working Group are explicitly engaging with anarchist theory and practice. Anarchism is not an afterthought.

It is openly, actively, and centrally present within Working Group activities and discussions. Participants engage with anarchist ideas and analysis and develop anarchistic forms of organizing and interrelating in activist projects.

Students involved with the Working Group have been inspired to do innovative research uncovering hidden histories of anarchist contributions to criminology as a discipline. This work has been presented at numerous conferences and been taken up by scholars elsewhere who have been provoked or encouraged by the Working Group students' works.

Thus the Working Group shows one way in which organizing within a specific academic discipline at a post-secondary institution, even a polytechnic labor market oriented one, can have a subversive impact with real world effects counter to those promoted by the institution and government.

# CHAPTER 11

# Defending Ourselves and Our Communities: Anarchist Self-Defense

The rising tide of fascism and organized political violence of the Right, particularly the mobilization of street level forces such as the Soldiers of Odin and the Oathkeepers has returned the question of self-defense to the center of anarchist and antifascist concerns. This concern has become perhaps more burning following the brutal fascist mobilization, and violence, enacted in Charlottesviille, Virginia, including the murder of Heather Hayer by a neo-Nazi. That anarchists and antifascists have been attacked with force at demonstrations (as in Vancouver and Seattle, where an antifascist syndicalist was shot) has made this a pressing concern. That regular folks intervening against racist violence on a Portland transit train were stabbed and killed by an openly identified white supremacist has made the issue of self-defense one of life or death importance. The killing of Heather Hayer shows that this murderous Rightwing violence is not isolated or about to diminish.

In Vancouver, as one example, unfortunately, in the absence of organized and effective self-defense formations, antifascists have had to rely on union flying squad members for defense at rallies. While this is fine up to a point and shows the significance and necessity of flying squads, it means that the antifascists became dependent on groupings of which they are not integrally a part (even if their interests are the same and they work in solidarity).

The present period shows up the inescapable necessity of anarchists engaging in self-defense training. But is shows too that this is not enough if it remains on an individual basis. The current context of rising tides of alt-Right threats underscores the need for community self-defense on a collective and organized basis.

In Surrey, British Columbia, where I live and work, Soldiers of Odin, an explicitly white supremacist and violent grouping, have taken to trying to build connections with homeless people at the homeless encampment on the so-called Strip. This is both an effort to counter the organizing work being done by anarchists and libertarian socialists on the Strip as well as an attempt to stir up opposition to recent refugees from Syria, many of whom have been settled in Surrey, the province's fastest growing city, since 2016.

The Soldiers of Odin are whipping up anti-migrant fear and anger by claiming that migrants are getting preferential treatment and access to housing that would otherwise go to homeless locals who have spent in some cases years on the streets in desperate need of housing. This is a myth in terms of government provision of housing for the homeless. It also, and fundamentally, serves to shift righteous anger and discontent away from the government, at all levels, and developers, where it actually belongs, and to direct it toward refugees who are blameless in the housing crisis in British Columbia. Thus it serves to divide the working class, poor, and marginalized against each other.

With the open movement of fascist shock troops like the Soldiers of Odin into areas in which anarchists are organizing, the need for organized self-defense is clear. Soldiers of Odin are showing up in larger numbers at times and are more ready, willing, and prepared to fight than are the anarchists and antifascists at this point.

In Vancouver, antifascist and anarchist groups have been attacked by fascists and white supremacists on more than one occasion. In one case an anarchist space was physically attacked. That space has been a center for organizing anarchist and antifascist projects, classes, and events as well as providing a space for discussion of insurrectionary and antifascist perspectives.

In another situation a rally of antifascists was attacked by Soldiers of Odin in downtown Vancouver. In that case Vancouver police intervened before the union defense squad could get to the fascists. The police once again played the role of protecting fascist aggressors while also intimidating antifascist organizers. That particular attack raised pointedly and in sharp focus the need for anarchist and antifascists to have organized collective defense at events as well as for individual members to have some self-defense training.

1      Black Blocs

Among the best known and most familiar forms of self-defense among anarchists in recent years has been the black bloc tactic. The black bloc originated as a means of self-defense against fascists and police in Germany in the 1980s. It provided crucial defense for squats which were subject to disruption or attack from fascists and police.

The black bloc tactic came to North America most prominently during the Active Resistance 96 counter-convention demonstration against the Democratic National Convention in Chicago in 1996 (Shantz 1998). There the black bloc opposed the official protocols that attempted to corral protesters into so-called protest pits well away from the convention site where they could be both contained and ignored and rendered irrelevant.

The black bloc then as now offers protection against identification by those who would harm anarchists. It prevents police from easily criminalizing anarchists. It also keeps fascists from identifying anarchists in order to inflict physical violence against them should they see them in the neighborhood.

Obviously, the black bloc in North America has been highly effective in street demos and protests. It does not translate so directly to regular, day to day, neighborhood self-defense. Clearly, wearing a mask or black bandana is not the best way to introduce or ingratiate yourself to your neighborhood and your neighbors. The anonymity that is so necessary in street demonstrations is counter-productive, even self-defeating, in the context of neighborhood solidarity building and self-defense.

## 2    ARA: Anti-Racist Action

Anarchist organizing against fascists and white supremacist groups in the period from the 1980s through the early 2000s was largely carried out in the form of Anti-Racist Action (ARA). ARA groupings were active in numerous cities in North America. In Canada there were active ARA chapters in Toronto, Montreal, and Calgary.

ARA was organized largely as a reactive street fighting force of anti-racists who were willing to put their bodies on the line to confront fascists when they met publicly or to oppose fascists at events, like concerts. Rather than a systematically organized and well trained fighting force or structured self-defense force, ARA was made up of committed and personally driven folks ready to fight to break up meetings of fascists. While individual members of ARA would do martial arts training it was not the case that ARA did systematic training. It was also not the case that they organized on the basis of defense formations. Action tended to be more spontaneous and reactive.

ARA did also often provide guards for events such as protests or demonstrations by groups like anti-poverty activists. They also did educational work through free schools and anarchist conferences as well as hosting numerous well attended concerts and festivals to raise awareness and funds for social movements. ARA worked in solidarity with and could be counted on to do some guardianship for anti-poverty groups like the Ontario Coalition Against Poverty.

The threat of fascist and white supremacist violence is always a present one in capitalist societies. While attention has rightly been given to recent acts of lethal violence against anti-racists, it is often forgotten that ARA suffered losses of its own a generation ago. In 1998 two ARA activists Lin "Spit" Newborn and Daniel Shersty were killed by fascists in Las Vegas.

## 3      The Nature of Policing

One of the outcomes of organized confrontation with fascists, in addition to putting down fascists movements before they can consolidate, is that it reveals openly the real sympathies that police forces have with fascists. This was a reality that came painfully to the fore for many in Charlottesville, Virginia during the Unite the Right assault. Many liberal commentators were surprised that police stood by while neo-Nazis roamed throughout the city core, often attacking people while police stood by. Armed militias marched through the streets and police did nothing. In the case of DeAndre Harris neo-Nazis bat the African American youth in a parking garage near the police center. Notably the assault was broken up by antifascists.

In one instance that I was involved in with ARA we confronted a meeting of neo-Nazis taking place in an old hotel in a gentrifying section of Queen Street West in Toronto, the Gladstone Hotel. Dozens of neo-Nazis were assembled in the back room pool area of the bar. We confronted them, unfortunately with smaller numbers, in order to get them out of the bar. This included telling the bar staff and patrons that Nazis were meeting in and using the bar as an organizing space.

Tellingly, some would say incredibly but it was not surprising, as the Nazis were preparing to leave, Toronto police officers showed up and instead of escorting the Nazis out (which we were certainly happy to do on our own) pushed ARA people out of the bar and threatened us with arrest. Toronto Police Service officers even went further. They pushed ARA people along Queen Street away from the hotel so we could not re-enter to ensure the Nazis left (which police did not insist they do). The police instead stayed at the hotel, with officers stationed outside so that the Nazis could go about continuing their rounds of pool matches and their organizing meetings without being disturbed any further.

## 4      Copwatch

For some anarchists another self-defense practice has taken the form of copwatch patrols. Copwatching involves the organized sousveillance—that is grassroots observation from below of authorities as opposed to the top down surveillance of non-elites by authorities—of police officers, particularly in working class neighborhoods.

In Surrey we have initiated copwatching crews to record, document, and publicize the violent actions of Royal Canadian Mounted Police (RCMP) officers and bylaw enforcement officers against homeless people on the Strip. This has included documentation of police and bylaw stealing and destroying the personal belongings of homeless people. As these actions have been publicized police have changed their actions considerably being less abusive of residents of the Strip. At least one bylaw enforcement officer has been canned as a result of publicized activities against homeless people (trashing belongings).

Copwatch is at once a means of inhibiting police violence, recording police violence, and making police feel uncomfortable in their work. It can act as self-defense in obstructing or interfering with normal police operations.

On one hand it impedes the regular functioning of police as agents of unaccountable discretionary (biased, unequal, unjust, oppressive) violence. On the other hand, it provides a counter-hegemonic representation of actual police practices against the presentations that police prefer to put forward as their public image. These include the practices of violence that police deny or which is never otherwise brought to light in the first place. In many poor and working class communities, especially racialized communities, the greatest threat that requires an organized defense comes from police officers.

The limitation of copwatching is that it does not fully contest the power and authority of police or challenge their capacity to operate. Rather it operates on the basis of whistleblowing or shaming specific officers or forces. In this it can have some impact. It does provide some impetus for officers to operate in a manner perhaps less ruthless than they might otherwise. It can also provide some support, assistance, or encouragement to people who are targeted by police.

Police violence happens in many cases because people targeted by police are alone. Policing in the streets at night targets street involved people who are often very much isolated.

Know your rights workshops educate people about practices and procedures to take when confronted by police (Austin 2000, 217). Role playing can be used to give people some experiences in effective responses to real world situations they can face in police encounters. Pamphlets with basic information about people's rights as well as names and contact information for legal and community organizations that can assist people (with legal counsel, filing complaints, etc.) can be provided.

Anarchists explicitly identify police as protectors of property rather than people in oppressed communities. Police violence is systemic, not a matter of "bad apples" and criminal justice reforms. Policing is the armed deployment of the state to contain and regulate populations. Its role and structure is military (Shantz 2017). It is the military arm of the capitalist state, in Austin's words (2000, 217). Police violence is not an unfortunate outcome of protecting communities. Protection of communities is not the role or function of police.

## 5     Defense Trainings

Reliance on reactive or momentary defense is often the case in antifascist actions today where defense is carried out on a more responsive basis depending on the actions of fascists. Or in more free for all assaults on fascists as in frontal charges. There is little strategic or tactical preparation or discipline.

There have been over the years various projects for martial arts training among anarchist and antifascist activists, spaces, and communities in specific contexts. Anarchist free schools and free spaces have run martial arts trainings sessions.

At the Anarchist Free Space and Free Skool in Toronto, martial arts training was provided along with classes on anarchism and art, anarchist communism, Situationism, and introductory anarchist theory. Notably, perhaps, these training sessions were less frequently run and less well attended than the other courses. In fact there was some sense among Free Skool participants and collective members alike that the martial arts courses were less necessary or relevant that the theoretical and historical courses. They were even viewed as less important than other skills training courses. Indeed the art courses were better attended and more regularly offered. The pressing need that some recognize or feel right now was clearly not as widespread among Toronto anarchists at least.

At the same time the need for organized self-defense on a more systematic basis was not lost on all Toronto anarchists. In fact, one longtime member of the cyber anarchist collective TAO Communications who studied Aikido was persistent in trying to organize Aikido classes for anarchists. Eventually he would broaden his vision into a dojo that trained anarchists as well as, eventually, youth from racialized communities in working class neighborhoods in Toronto. In fact the dojo was set up not far from the Gladstone Hotel, where the neo-Nazis had met some time earlier.

## 6     An Existing Model: Flying Squads and Self-Defense

An anarchist defense squad could be trained and organized in virtually any locale. Training would work on the basis of practical skill sharing that anarchists have used on other issues from micro-radio to gardens, to computers.

Fascist times are periods of open, brutal, class war (when the sheets quite literally slip off). Events of the last year, including the killing of three people opposing a white supremacist harassing racialized women on a transit train in Portland and the murder of Heather Heyer by a neo-Nazi in Charlottesville, show the desperate need for working class self-defense of our communities.

In this we can draw on examples of rank-and-file self-defense organization. I would suggest, in particular, the rank and file flying squad provides an existing model for a rapid mobilization defense force for community protection.

I grew up in an autoworker family and in my family union, UAW (then CAW, now UNIFOR) Local 444 there was a very active and militant flying squad. It was deployed to defend workers and the community against a range of social threats, including, of course, during strikes, but beyond. In Toronto, CAW flying squads were mobilized to defend immigrants and people facing deportation. Flying squads also defended unemployed workers and homeless people from attacks by police and Rightist vigilantes during protests and demonstrations. A rank-and-file CUPE (Canadian Union of Public Employees) flying squad mobilized to defend Indigenous land protectors against racist mobs.

The structural basis for a defense squad organization is already provided by the example of the union flying squad. A defense force could be mobilized quickly through a phone list accessible to all members. Not only does the flying squad framework allow for quick deployment. It also builds on pre-existing relationships of trust and action. The flying squad members know each other and have important experiences working together during political actions, protests, and/or workplace strikes and pickets. Flying squads have experiences of and familiarity with direct action. The flying squad members also typically have relationships of activity and trust with people in other social movements and community groups, such as anti-poverty groups or migrant defense groups. Such was the case in Toronto with various, both union based and autonomous, flying squads and relationships with the Ontario Coalition Against Poverty.

The flying squad structure operates along the lines of affinity groups with which anarchists are so familiar and which many prefer. The structure allows members to know each other's strengths and weaknesses, preferences and discomforts. The active relationships of the flying squad reinforce accountability and commitment.

In Toronto, anarchists, some of whom were workers, some of whom were union members, formed an autonomous flying squad. The autonomous flying squad was organized typically to do strike support for striking workers on picket lines. Flying squad members could engage in activities, such as violating injunctions or strike protocols, that the striking workers did not feel they could do. The autonomous flying squad also mobilized for support for community groups during political actions.

In Vancouver, unionists have organized a self-defense unit, the Peacekeepers. They train together and organize to defend protesters against opponents including fascist groups such as the Soldiers of Odin. This is one model of mobile self-defense organizing that combines explicit self-defense with a flying squad structure for rapid mobilization and coordinated action.

In some cases flying squad members, as members of unions, can draw on additional established working class resources, such as legal support and defense funds for members who might need them based on their flying squad self-defense activities. These resources might not be available to more precarious or vulnerable people who might be targeted by fascists or police.

As self-defense practices spread, other groupings can take on some of these roles but the flying squad offers an already existing body of workers ready, willing and able to do some of the work of self-defense.

The uses of such a defense force will depend on local threats and issues. Training can be extended throughout a given community or neighborhood thus providing spaces and practices of solidarity building. On a larger basis they can provide alternatives to statist intrusions on communities. Doing so would, of course, involve developing self-defense on a broad, more regular, community basis.

In Vancouver, the IWW branch is making a possibly significant turn towards self-defense training and organizing to act as a defense squad for public mobilizations and potentially for community self-defense. But their numbers are small. A broader flying squad drawing on experiences and participation of already organized working class flying squads could provide more extensive defense.

7    **Community Defense**

Organized community self-defense is an aspect of social life that oppressed communities are regularly engaged in in addressing and improving their living conditions. This is a matter of community care and commitment to the generations, younger and older alike, that live in the communities. It is collective work, organized by definition.

Much radical community self-defense derives from the examples set by the Black Panther Party and other militant African American organizing efforts. The Black Panther Party organized police patrols, to follow and monitor police officers in African American communities, dealing with forces that very much acted like occupying armies in those communities that they were not part of and did not live in. The Black Panther Party patrols carried guns and copies of the California Penal Code detailing mandatory procedures of police in detaining people (Austin 2000, 218). Nowadays copwatching is done with videos and cell phones but the principle remains.

Richard Austin describes an earlier, but still recent, example. His work involved Forever in Struggle Together (FIST). FIST was a grassroots collective of people of African descent based in central Brooklyn.

FIST emerged out of the Student Power Movement (SPM) organized to address budget cuts in higher education in New York State in 1995 (Austin 2000, 215). SPM involved mass organizing among younger activists of color to oppose threats to the City University of New York (CUNY) system, especially funding cuts and threats to accessibility especially for African American students. It also spread to oppose the introduction of armed SAFE officers on campus. SPM also worked on support campaigns for political prisoner Mumia Abu Jamal, a death row prisoner and Black Panther Party member railroaded for the killing of a police officer in Philadelphia. SPM used political education, mass rallies, and direct action to press their issues.

Recognizing a need to move to rooted, longer term struggles as members graduated and left campuses, they developed FIST as a community based resistance organization. FIST was actively involved in community self-defense and education against police violence in their communities. FIST was especially involved in organizing alternative means of protecting communities, beyond the police (Austin 2000, 217).

FIST worked to develop stronger block and tenants associations with civilians patrols of their neighborhoods. The idea is for patrols to deter anti-social behavior and respond to people's fears and to real social threats within the community (Austin 2000, 219). This is different from patrols to harass youth for horseplay or to criminalize annoying behavior or disturbances or minor aspects of underground economies as current policing does. People's actions are addressed rather than demonizing the people themselves.

Community pressure, what criminologists refer to as informal social controls, can pressure people to stop anti-social behavior. Work is also done to create safe community spaces where people can congregate without fear in public. Communities develop codes of conduct on the streets. This involves cultural transmission of community norms, values, and beliefs and means listening to elders, to building intergenerational connections.

Conflict resolution is used to address disputes and interpersonal conflict and violence. This requires degrees of community trust. That trust can be built as people engage and convers with one another on the streets and in supporting community improvements or support.

It can prevent the violent interventions of police, but people have to participate in it and trust it. Mutual respect is key and can develop through open engagement (including respect of elders for youth and their views and under-standings) (Austin 2000, 219).

FIST has worked in the New York City Coalition against Police Brutality (CAPB) to resist racist police violence. It is a coalition of Black, Latino/a, Asian, and LGBTQ youth. These coalitions will offer examples of broader organizing for community organizing going forward.

Communities do need protecting. So there is a need for an organization *of the community* and *by the community*, organized to do that work.

Community self-defense is an important expression of mutual aid, the basic anarchist impulse and organizing principle. Self-defense on this basis moves beyond dependence on the state for protection or response to crisis. It helps people develop relationships, skills, and confidence to support community members rather than turning to the state. It also helps break the reflex response of looking to the state to address social problems or threats more broadly.

## 8      Conclusion

This remains very much an underdeveloped area of anarchist work, never mind broader community work. It is one that many anarchists are waking up to with some sense of urgency

One thing is becoming quite certain. That is that organized fascist and white supremacist groupings have a sizeable proportion of people who have martial arts and even, of course, military training. Many fascists in Canada display personal military markings openly and present their military background and training in an up front, in your face manner. This is true of fascist groupings in the United States as well. Members of the Oathkeepers, for example, have military and/or police training.

The military training, of course, goes hand in hand with weapons training. In the US, and perhaps increasingly in Canada, this goes along with the possession of firearms by members of organized fascist groups.

Anarchists have, or at least should not have, no illusions that in the present period they can satisfactorily meet community needs for self-defense. There is much work to be done and many cities with anarchist movements have minimal self-defense capacities. Yet this is a real challenge to anarchists. It is impossible to speak meaningfully of alternatives to the state and to provide compelling evidence to people that anarchism offers something of a realistic or practical alternative if these resources and capacities are not developed.

It does not provide a bridge from the current state of affairs to anarchism if such needs cannot be met in an anarchic manner. And it leaves people unconvinced. This is not to say that full self-defense capacities must be achieved. But more work needs to be done to approach an effective and compelling level of community care.

Self-defense efforts offer an important means for bringing non-anarchists into relationships with anarchists. People will become involved in self-defense efforts against fascists and/or against police violence even if they have not identified themselves as, or will not ever see themselves as, anarchists.

As in all of the efforts outlined in this book, the aim is beyond immediate defense issues to change the conditions that give rise to social harm in the first place. That means ownership of resources and exploitation. It means, in community issues, confronting bad bosses, slumlords, gentrifiers, developers, and real estate speculators. They should not be given free and open access to our communities and where they refuse to meet community standards and values, should be driven out. And communities need to develop mechanisms and capacities for doing so.

Communities must move toward liberation from the state and exploiters. Community control must be made a real prospect. And organizing geared toward this aim. Residents must develop collective capacities in our neighborhoods. This is self-determination in action. But it requires ongoing experiences and resources.

The examples outlined here allow for shared experiences and learning how to confront and deal with realities like police violence. There is a need for experiences in a range of community support work (from chairing a working group to community research to self-defense and direct action, etc.). These experiences develop capacities and increase confidence for people. People need to ensure the safety and security of their communities without turning to police.

CHAPTER 12

# A Wrap: Organizing Anarchism

Anarchists are doing serious organizing work across a range of issues and in various sites of key social struggles in the early decades of the twenty-first century, and in a context of political repression and active social war. They are working to organize workplaces or to radicalize workers within workplaces (organized or otherwise). They are organizing critical pedagogical spaces to share experiences of resistance or break through the hegemonic views, ideas, and practices that try to tell people that there is no alternative, no other possibility beyond state capitalist misery, crisis and anxiety. Anarchist organizing not only shows that another world is possible, it is providing necessary infrastructures for building that world here and now.

Anarchists are organizing to open up technological resources and expand technical knowledge to provide people with insights into the skills and knowledge behind the wired world, while also making technologies available to people who would otherwise lack access. They are challenging corporate and state claims on technological resources, knowledge, and relationships. They are re-emphasizing people as producers rather than only consumers or users.

Anarchists are organizing to support peoples' health, including emotional, mental and psychological as well as physical health. They are literally saving lives. At the same time they are re-centering health care within collective contexts rather than as matters of individual care and good, or bad, luck. This in contexts where many people lack access to decent health resources or are criminalized for personal health care behaviors. Anarchists are developing key knowledge that can contribute to better health possibilities while providing resources to lessen ill health outcomes.

Anarchists are organizing to challenge the corporatization and authoritarianism of neoliberal edu-factories and develop postsecondary institutions as resources and spaces of and for critical thinking, solidarity, and resistance. They are building new relationships and new practices for teaching and learning, for critical engagement, for turning ideas into action, and transforming social interactions.

Anarchists are organizing to provide collective self-defense and protection. This is crucial in a period of both rising fascist violence and ongoing (and even increasing) police violence against communities of the exploited and oppressed generally and against open opposition movements, including police attacks on protests and demonstrations against state capitalism and its institutions. This ongoing work is especially vital in the current context of emboldened far Right and fascist movements which have shown no hesitation in shooting anarchists and killing antifascists. This is an area of organizing work that historically anarchists have devoted serious time and attention to but which contemporary anarchists have perhaps overlooked until recently. Now they have no choice but to step up efforts in this regard. It has become something of a matter of self-preservation.

Anarchists are contesting and opposing the repressive apparatus of the state and capital and maintaining community relations of resistance in the face of criminalization. They are building connections of solidarity with prisoners and working to challenge the separation and isolation of criminalized members of communities in resistance.

All of these examples of anarchist organizing practice point to the seriousness of anarchist projects and of anarchists involved within them. They stand as living examples of anarchism in action. They show clearly that far from being a utopian movement of faraway or unrealizable dreams, anarchism is a highly practical social politics. Anarchists are not unrealistic dreamers (though dreams are vital to sustain any of us). Nor are anarchists armchair philosophers. They are not the impatient children or infantile idealists that their critics, both conservatives and Leftist radicals, have made them out to be.

Rather anarchists are engaged, serious, and thoughtful in their approach and experiential in their politics. Their approach is, as in the best traditions of political radicalism, rooted in the needs, concerns, and desires of people in the real world of everyday life. With an eye to a better future of alternative, caring, social relations.

It is also true that anarchists are not utopian in trying to impose a conceptual vision on a recalcitrant world. Anarchist organizing activities are tried in practice, revised, developed, expanded where it makes sense, and dropped where that is what is needed.

1    From Here to There: Survival Strategies, Insurrectionary
     Infrastructures, and Prefigurative Politics

It has been remarked by sociologically informed anarchists, from Paul Goodman and Colin Ward, that within archic, authoritarian societies people often lack experiences of non-hierarchical, non-authoritarian relationships in their social lives. From teachers to bosses to cops to media, etc. we are socialized to operate, trained to accept and to expect authoritarian structures. We are socialized and conditioned to take orders (and occasionally, toward someone with even less status or power than ourselves, to give them). Spaces for non-hierarchical relating, mutual aid, participatory and egalitarian decision making are too few and far between.

There are too few venues for people to come together to support one another, collectively identify and meet important community and personal needs, while at the same time pointing toward better alternative ways of doing things. Particularly in neoliberal times we are conditioned to see problems as individual problems (even as exclusively your own fault) or to accept diminished expectations or a sense that nothing else is possible, there is no alternative.

Anarchist organizing projects, regardless of venue, issue or emphasis, are spaces in which we can re-introduce ourselves to non-authoritarian relationships. Where we can practice non-authoritarian decision making. Where we can develop mutual aid and trust. And where we can do so without fearing a penalty imposed for our honest and innocent mistakes. These projects are prefigurative in this sense. And they afford us opportunities to learn together, to share experiences and lessons, and to improve and refine our practices and our visions of the possible and the preferable.

Anarchist projects occupy spaces between the meeting of daily needs today and prefiguring new ways of living tomorrow. They are concerned with day to day needs of survival with strategies and tactics for social change, struggle, and resistance, while being creatively and experimentally prefigurative. They show glimpses of an anarchist future of new ways of relating socially, while addressing pressing concerns in the structure of the old society. They offer a glimpse of, as some have called it, the new world in the shell of the old.

The organizing projects of anarchism discussed here show the great variety of work being done by anarchists to build infrastructures of resistance. These are the resources and frameworks for sustaining people and struggles in the current context while providing larger forces of transformation for both the near and distant future. They allow for the durability and persistence of struggles over the longer term. Rather than being left responding to crises and challenges as they arise these infrastructures of resistance allow for strategic and tactical revisioning of struggles and for a movement of struggles, from defensive or reactive to offensive and directional, and affirmative.

Anarchists have sought, but struggled, to build capacities for sustenance and struggle within communities of the working class. This is an aspect of what the Black Panthers referred to as "survival pending revolution." And anarchists do not, as some critics might contend, the revolution—often conceived in insurrectionist terms. At the same time we do not want to suggest that only anarchists are working to build these capacities. Clearly they are not alone. The emphasis here is rather on the specific organizing works that anarchists are doing as anarchists.

## 2    Not a Party

Anarchist organizing has differed from other far Left organizing in eschewing the organizational form of the vanguard party. Anarchists have, of course, not been party builders and have not oriented their organizing toward building membership based groups geared toward the seizure of the state ate any level in any way (whether social democratic parliamentarianism or revolutionary state control in the form of a coup or a dictatorship of the proletariat).

One might note that there are no chapters here on cadre based organizations or vanguard groups of political theorists or self-decided "revolutionaries." That is not the aim of the book and it is not the aim of anarchist organizers. That is not what they are building.

Organizing cannot, as many 1960s movements did, lose connections to the broader social sectors among the working class. Ideological purity comes from detachment. Strategies and tactics must evolve in practice over changing contexts. Ritualism and formulaic approaches must be avoided and/or abandoned.

The 1960s movement veterans recognized that lulls in mass protest were coming and realized the need to prepare for it. Many made the decision, fatally perhaps, to build vanguard cadre based organizations as their means to carry resistance through the foreseen low periods.

Today, we can and must recognize the possibilities of ebbs in movement energies, even as we are in a period of upswing in mobilizations. But our conclusions must lead us not to build vanguard circles but to build infrastructures that can be accessed and used by broader sections of the exploited and oppressed to meet daily needs while supporting future alternatives in the making.

In the manner of the evangelicals we might build organizations that provide some material essentials while also sustaining people emotionally and psychologically and providing perspectives on the world we want to realize and strategies and tactics for getting there. Dedication is not enough. Nor are audacity. Or "right" ideas. Economic structures and conditions, social relations, cultural socialization, all frame possibilities. Does history have shortcuts?

This is not about adopting an anarchist or radical identity. Key instead are what I have termed infrastructures of resistance. As Marxist historian and activist Max Elbaum puts it in reflecting on the lessons learned from the 1960s radical movements of which he was a part:

> Radicals must strain every nerve to gain and keep a connection to these millions [of working class people]. We need a connection in life, sustained over time, through durable organizations and institutions—not merely in theory or in self conception or during brief moments of high tide protest. This places a premium on resisting all sectarianism and flexibly adapting to new and often unexpected conditions. (2006, xiii)

Sometimes we will need to be more defensive to maintain and sustain ideas in tough periods. But we must still work to provide spaces for connections. As Elbaum continues: "But recognizing limits on the scope of our immediate practice must not harden into accepting marginal status as a permanent fact of life—much less a mindset that glorifies marginality as a sign of true revolutionary faith" (2006, xiii).

We need to build out of comfortable activist enclaves and bubbles.

## 3      Beyond Social Movement Frameworks

Anarchist movements do not easily fall within and cannot be contained by the typical or familiar frameworks of social movements theorizing within sociology. They are not geared toward seizure of the state, whether electorally through campaigns or policy reforms, or in the manner of a revolutionary party apparatus. The do not measure success by conventional means in terms of electoral victories, policy reforms, or social democratic services or welfare state provisions within a state capitalist context reproductive of systemic imperatives.

This does not mean that anarchist are completely agnostic. Indeed, they may support policy gains (rent controls, social assistance, education spending) or specific campaigns tactically or as means of defending sections of the population facing negative impacts from specific politicians, parties, or policy changes. They may even act electorally, as individuals, to block a reactionary candidate or party. They do not view these actions as positive gains or ends in themselves but view them as defensive maneuvers.

The structures of anarchist movements cannot be viewed in relation to these conventional political outcomes (access to politicians, reforms, or seizure of state power). As anarchist practice has always sought to do, contemporary anarchists move beyond and against these limited approaches and visions.

The diversity of anarchist projects within a context of a shared political vision offers broadly a different way of thinking about social movements. Not only in terms of going beyond state-centric or state capture approaches. They also break false divides between prefigurative and realist movements, even, perhaps, between revolution and reform. The emphasis on survival pending revolution spurs a rethinking of how social movements pursue alternative, transformative futures while making immediate changes and meeting social needs in the material conditions of current life.

At the same time, anarchist social movements are not motivated primarily by changes in values, postmaterial or otherwise, as New Social Movements theories would emphasize. Anarchist movements are organized around many so-called old social movement concerns—exploitation, workplace control, anti-poverty, housing, health care, etc. Yet they are expressive of alternative values and principles and involve campaigns for ecology, anti-racism, gender and sexual freedoms, alternative cultures, etc.

Anarchist projects are organized to develop and share resources for social transformations that bring these struggles together. In critically organizing, anarchists seek to transform social values in their projects and in society more broadly. So, for example, flying squads of rank-and-file workers may seek to overcome gender oppressions socially and in their collective work. And these will be viewed as interlinked parts of developing working class solidarity against exploitation and the power of owners and managers to divide and weaken working people. And this is part of a broader understanding of working class community health and wellbeing.

In anarchist organizing projects many of the false dichotomies of social movement analysis are superceded or dissolved. Anarchist movements are simultaneously economic, political, social, and cultural. They are oriented toward human and ecological justice.

Anarchist movements and projects offer important alternatives in contexts where alternative visions of social relations are lacking and too often constrained within reformist frameworks and electoral dead ends. Resistance in the age of post-Trump reaction must go beyond a rebound to neo-liberal or social democratic parties and appeals to lesser evilism. But many movements still struggle to pose in very real terms the sorts of strategies and tactics, programs and principles, that would really change economic, political, social, and cultural systems, structures, and relations in meaningful ways. Few movements pose a challenge to the existing balance of power as currently constituted, even in the limited spheres of municipal politics. In building radical infrastructures of resistance anarchists at least start from the perspective that a new world is not only desirable but possible.

They are also working to build some shared resources and organizational capacities toward that end. And they are doing so not as a means to elect better, or slightly less worse, rulers or to turn back the clock to a supposed social democratic golden age. Rather, they are trying to turn the calendar pages forward.

This is not to say that they have solved all of the problems they set out to solve within their own organizing practices. Or even that they have posed all of the problems or posed them properly. If anarchists have not stamped out racism, sexism, transphobia, etc. in society, it is also true and must be acknowledged that anarchist projects still struggle with their own failings lack of development in these areas.

## 4      Some Pitfalls

There are some pitfalls, limitations or gaps, in anarchist organizing. On the one hand, the decentralized approaches to anarchist organizing can lead to weakened capacities to coordinate offensive struggles. Anarchists, at present, are good at meeting some needs and doing some sustenance work and even defensive efforts. Anarchists have been less effective at organizing offensive struggles and have certainly been limited in maintaining sustained offensives against states or capital.

In addition, the "big tent" approach of much anarchist politics and synthesist tendencies within anarchism have hindered capacities to develop and disseminate anarchist perspectives more broadly in struggles and has perhaps contributed to the limiting of capacities to develop coordinated offensive struggles. Synthesism tends toward lowest common denominator anarchism (only those projects with consensus are undertaken) and, while bringing anarchists together, generally weakens anarchist focus within organizing campaigns in broader movements or struggle contexts.

The general approach in anarchism can leave non-anarchists confused about anarchist principles and allow anarchists to be undermined or sidelined by more unified Leftist groups who have developed closeness, and focus, in theory and practice.

Anarchist organizing has also been susceptible to what Jo Freeman has called the tyranny of structurelessness. Not forming groups with formal leadership structures, roles, and responsibilities does not mean that these do not develop within anarchist groups in practice (and worse). The lack of formal or collectively agreed upon structures and processes, including structures and processes of accountability, can lead anarchist groups to default to leadership by the most active or most popular or most articulate. It can default to those with the most available time or resources (and not provide time or resources equitably to people involved in organizing work). It can also substitute leadership by the elected with the leadership of unelected cliques or circles. In place of leadership cadres, leadership cliques. This can develop an "ad hocracy" (bureaucracy on an ad hoc basis).

Cultural or subcultural capital, or privilege, can determine positions within group actions and roles. People can be "voted out" through whisper campaigns and cold shouldering rather than an actual open vote with accountable processes. Status and prestige systems based on personal characteristics and personality can emerge and become entrenched. Some can be marginalized simply because they do not comfortably or conventionally express activist lingo or cultural valuations, or speaking patterns, or even modes of self-carriage.

At the same time the less popular, or less active, or less articulate, or less outgoing, or less self-promoting, can be relegated to marginal positions or excluded. Personality circles or cliques can become unstated and unacknowledged central committees. This can be exacerbated if affinity groups become collective houses where decisions are made outside of, beyond, in addition to, or against the actual projects that people are involved in (including those outside the affinity group), like a free space, for example.

You can openly confront and replace the people occupying formal roles, through agreed upon and accountable processes, or contest decisions made in formal decision making structures, which all members are notified of and can participate in. It becomes murkier to do so in less formal groupings that might not even acknowledge their own existence.

This is not to excuse formal group structures or suggest that they do not have serious problems (many of which anarchists rightly identify and attempt to provide alternatives to). It is rather to recognize that anarchist organizations are not free of their own challenges simply by claiming to be anarchist or by suggesting that they are automatically better than non-anarchist organizational structures.

## 5    Participation Problems

Anarchist movements and projects still face various issues of membership, participation, and composition. There are ongoing problems of inclusion and accessibility. There is much to do to break anarchist movements out of subcultural circles or alternative cultural spaces. This includes reaching out beyond those who have made up much of anarchist projects over the last few decades in North America, for example. These projects have been relatively limited in terms of composition, experiences, outlook.

Anarchist movements are still largely white in member composition in many if not most contexts. There remain serious issues with male dominance, sexism, sexual violence, and gendered divisions of labor. Trans-exclusionism continues to be problematic in specific contexts.

At the same time many anarchist scenes are decidedly declasse middle strata in character rather than being spaces of working class people, cultures, references. Many come from middle strata backgrounds and have enjoyed advanced educational opportunities and experiences. Anarchists need to be careful not to be exclusionary in speech, cultural assumptions, theoretical orientations.

Anarchist projects still struggle to address their settler character on Indigenous lands and to work as allies in anti-colonial and decolonizing movements and projects. There is much work that can be done in struggles to defend the land, to end colonial institutions, like the criminal justice institutions, to confront colonial states and extractives industries.

There is still much to be done in terms of reaching out beyond the circles of anarchist movements to meet and engage with folks for whom anarchism is misunderstood or not understood at all. It is safe to say that many or most in society have little familiarity with histories of anarchism and that still fewer have much awareness of anarchist projects.

For many, anarchism is a mystery. Caricatures of anarchism as chaos, disorder, or terrorism, the staples of state and mass media presentations of anarchism are still common currency. And what first hand experiences do people have with anarchism in action to dispel these caricatures and distortions?

Well, that is the work that anarchists still have a lot to do and much to overcome. As anarchists expand their projects and make themselves felt in relevant ways in their neighborhoods and communities these understandings will shift. My experiences have been that many come to see anarchism as serious and useful in a short period of time when they have exposure to anarchist projects and anarchist organizers in action.

6    Against Colonialism and Borders: Building Bridges

Anarchists have innovated a range of flexible practices, responsive to changing social circumstances and structural conditions. They have built, and are building, a variety of spaces in, through, and for organizing in diverse, though still largely urban, contexts. These practices and spaces both meet specific needs of participants and community members more extensively on a day to day basis while also providing opportunities to build bridges with non-anarchists and broader communities of people with differing degrees of politicization.

Despite this, there remain a number of serious challenges for anarchist organizing. These include working to build bridges across communities not familiar with, conversant in, or converted to anarchist perspectives and anarchist organizing. Much of the working class remains disconnected from, unfamiliar with, and even wary of anarchism. This is in no way surprising given the extreme efforts exerted by economic and political powerholders to disparage and distort anarchism as chaos and disorder and to pose anarchism as something to fear. Added to this is the great pleasure corporate mass media take in presenting anarchism primarily in the form of riot porn or decontextualized images of street fights. Yet anarchists have a responsibility to break through this by example—by making their work useful and relevant and by breaking out of the margins to engage directly with people in their communities.

Bridges must be built to people facing growing threats from the state and capital, and their vigilantes among the far Right. This includes the pressing need to develop migrant defense against border security, detention, and deportation. This can include defending people against ICE sweeps, anti-terror law targeting and detentions, and against the demonization of migrants publicly. Projects that anarchists can (and in some places are) engage include deportation defenses, building a new underground railroad for displaced people, safe houses and sanctuary, etc. Some work has been started on these and other efforts and I have written about some earlier efforts toward these ends (in the early 2000s context elsewhere, see Shantz 2010).

Another area in which anarchists need to do much work to catch up is in anti-colonial struggles and in solidarity with the Indigenous communities across Turtle Island on whose lands settler anarchists live, work, and organize. Anarchists have begun this work and many anarchists collectives take it seriously (even if their material efforts remain limited, and developing), Still anarchist organizing is nowhere near where it needs to be in doing this work and anarchists still have a lot to learn—in their own education and in listening to (really listening to) Indigenous people.

Indeed, the Left in general is behind where it should be in anti-colonial work and that reflects effects of colonialism and the gaps in Leftist practice and thought. The disconnection between anarchists and anti-colonial struggles and migrant struggles points to the whiteness of much of the anarchist circles in North America and the gaps in anarchist, and Leftist, theories historically.

Work can be done, as allies, taking direction from Indigenous communities, in land defense, anti-racism, defense against state violence (police courts, corrections), and against violence by Right wing and fascist groups. It can include actions against extractives industries and extreme energy projects, as many anarchists are learning to do in contexts like the unceded Indigenous territories at so-called British Columbia.

Allies need to mobilize to counter settler racists in communities near where self-determined Indigenous actions are taking place. For example, during a land reclamation at Six Nations, near Toronto, I was involved with a group of settlers who went door to door in the nearby settler town of Caledonia to talk directly to non-Indigenous people about the just nature of the reclamation and to confront and challenge the settler townspeople's often racist assumptions about the Six Nations communities, land reclaimers, and their efforts. Tough work but necessary. Settlers could do that work in a context that would have been violent, extremely so, for Indigenous people. And it allowed the land defenders to focus on their work, not on explaining it to often hostile settlers.

That work involved its own challenges among settler anarchists too. Many preferred the "cool" setting of the occupation site, and the center of action, and were not comfortable challenging other settlers face to face. This type of organizing by definition pushes settler anarchists to leave their comfort zones. And it shows them up front the violence faced by Indigenous people on their own land. Not doing this work is abdicating responsibility, by white settler anarchists, in a context of settler colonialism and white supremacy.

This organizing work is crucial for anti-capitalist activists because it reminds them too that the nature of capitalism is enclosure of land and sustenance and the displacement of non-elites generally. This is a point of commonality for all of the exploited and oppressed. We have all been victimized by dispossession and displacement. We are all rendered migrant by capital in various ways.

Structural challenges remain. Divisions within the working class, the dominance of the two party system in the United States and first past the post electoralism in the US and Canada, and the economic, political, and technical resources of capital, pose ongoing (even growing) challenges to even the most organized anarchist movements as currently constituted. No insurrectionary care will reverse the course of US or Canadian politics under these circumstances. That there is no global counterforce elsewhere to break the US dominated global capitalist market is also a factor.

But cracks in state capitalist dominance are showing (if not yet fissures). Energy crises and the opposition to extractives by Indigenous communities pressing decolonization. Uprisings in key areas, in the Middle East, for example.

Global migration. These all pose challenges to liberal democratic and capitalist hegemony.


## 7    More to be Done

Anarchists still need to develop work on issues of class, exploitation, and control of resources and organize on a class wide basis. Expropriating the expropriators must become "a thing" again. And anarchists must dedicate energies to build capacities to do it. As this work shows, anarchists are undertaking important and interesting initiatives in organizing at work among people directly at the site of exploitation. Yet much work needs to be done to develop class awareness, class consciousness, and class action—and anarchists need to play parts in this. For too long, perhaps, anarchists have shunned class analysis or viewed themselves as somehow declasse or against class (while still constrained within systems of class like jobs, and rent). They need to recognize and confront their place as laborers (manual, mental, emotional, whatever) within labor markets who need to sell themselves in order to survive and who are alienated from the labor they expend and value they create within ongoing systems of extraction of labor.

Many younger anarchists have extensive experiences in new industries (tech, service, virtual, etc.) and have much to teach older anarchists about new and emerging sectors. They also have specific skills in communicating with their cohort of workers in these industries.

Anarchists in North American have much to do to develop organizational capacities in areas of pressing significance for the exploited and oppressed. These areas and issues include housing, for one. Anarchists in North America are well behind anarchists in parts of Europe like Exarchia in Greece or in Copenhagen or in Berlin. In those contexts anarchists can claim entire neighborhoods. Nothing of the sort quite exists in North America. I have written on anarchist efforts around housing, particularly some specific squatting initiatives, elsewhere. One can refer to my earlier work in Constructive Anarchy on squatting efforts in Toronto. More, much more, needs to be done.

One of the things conservative religious orders have done is to support working class people in housing. Anarchists need to do this, especially given the impossible housing situations in cities like Vancouver and Toronto, for example. Housing and homelessness have been key issues of our times and are only growing in severity and impact as cities like Vancouver become unlivable for all but the most wealthy or as people turn to "options" like boats, cars, and trailers.

Anarchists still need to move beyond movementist practices, as many have and are doing, to be sure, on a broader basis. There are still tendencies to organize in anarchist enclaves or on more insular projects. Workplace organizing can help anarchists to break out of this constraint. So too can organizing around health care issues.

Anarchist organizing moves between tensions toward a need for maintaining and developing explicitly anarchist perspectives, strategies, and tactics to avoid a watering down into liberalism or reformism (or single cause campaigns) or get along consensus and, on the other hand, an isolating purity or a comfortable hobbyism.

## 8       Conclusions

The projects discussed in detail here show the creativity and commitment of anarchist organizers and the viability of anarchist organizing. They provide real world examples that make clear that another world is both possible and in the making, even if in small, initial, steps.

These projects are perhaps best understood as infrastructures that might provide bases of sustenance and continued, broadening, struggle. They are not utopian models that can re/make the world on their own and they are not substitutions for developing an alternative society. Broader changes in the economy, structures of labor and production, etc. Will provide new forms of social relationships and social interchange. While it is true that history cannot be forced, it is also true that it can be urged along, even given a shove.

These organizing efforts will provide supports and resources as people in broader numbers shift the balance of forces and reorganize social life in relation to changes in labor processes, production relations, etc.

There are always challenges to avoid sectarianism, unrealistic strategies and tactics, voluntarism, and anti-democratic practices. To these can be added moralism and identity exclusiveness (as "radicals," etc.). And the self-righteousness that condemning people's mistakes of learning and confuses rudeness or carelessness for oppression. And seeks to oust every form of personal foible for insensitivity from the movement (on a guise of "anti-oppression").

There remains a need to develop durable organizational links to larger working class bases. And a need for patience and understanding and compassion.

Of great significance, historian of the Sixties movements Max Elbaum notes that radical anti-capitalist movements like the New Communist Movement of the 1970s left virtually no institutional legacy of which future generations could grow and build. This left a break in infrastructures between the New Left movement radicalism and the generations of activists radicalized in the late-1990s and in the alternative globalization uprisings, for example.

Conditions are never what we would like them to be. Yet as analysts of the New Left, including Elbaum, suggest, the New Left squandered important opportunities it did have. Among these were consolidating radical trends and offering some institutional stability for galvanizing broader, popular resistance (Elbaum 2006, 7). They could have provided poles around which resistance forces might have coalesced and been sustained. That is one of the challenges that confronts anarchists today. Movements must grow roots within communities of the exploited and the oppressed. Gains made in periods of upswing must be preserved in durable and resilient bases.

The Left lacks a mass base or deep roots in working class life. The Left and the working class are divided along racialized lines. Organizational models, strategies, and tactics are lacking and in need of a rethinking. But as the examples in this work show, anarchists are offering some lively, vital, serious, and promising answers. And they are actively revising and reworking those answers as the lessons of practice suggest to them.

Some habits are hard to change. Many anarchists still believe that the effectiveness of politics is a function of their excitement or whether they are "fun" or not. Many disparage the hard work of organizing as being boring or want to believe that playfulness trumps the labor necessary to sustain revolt (which is also work in its own way). And some believe still, despite the lessons of the 1960s and 1970s, that commitment and revolutionary inspiration can be enough—that insurrection can be sparked by inspiring acts of revolt alone—by a contemporary form of propaganda of the deed.

# Bibliography

Adam, Barry D. 1978. *The Survival of Domination: Inferiorization and Everyday Life*. New York: Elsevier.

Anderson, Harlene. 1997. *Conversation, Language and Possibilities: A Postmodern Approach to Therapy*. New York: Basic Books.

Anonymous. 2013. "What do We Learn in School that Couldn't be Learned Elsewhere?" *Fifth Estate* 47(3): 25–27.

Austin, Richard. 2000. "Under the Veil of Suspicion: Organizing Resistance and Struggling for Liberation." In *Police Brutality*, Jill Nelson (ed.). New York: WW Norton, 206–223.

Barnes, Marian. 1999. "Users as Citizens: Collective Action and the Local Governance of Welfare." *Social Policy and Administration* 33(1): 73–90.

Cantril, Hadley. 1941. *The Psychology of Social Movements*. New York: Wiley.

Clastres, Pierre. 1989. *Society Against the State: Essays in Political Anthropology*. Boston: Zone Books.

Clastres, Pierre. 2010. *Archaeology of Violence*. New York: Semiotext(e).

Cohen, J. 1985. "Strategy or Identity: New Theoretical Paradigms and Contemporary Social Movements." *Social Research* 52(4): 663–716.

Coleman, Gabriella. 2014. *Hacker, Hoaxer, Whistleblower, Spy: The Many Faces of Anonymous*. London: Verso.

Crossley, N. 1999. "Working Utopias and Social Movements: An Investigation Using Case Study Materials from Radical Mental Health Movements in Britain." *Sociology* 33(4): 809–830.

D'Arcus, Bruce. 2013. *Boundaries of Dissent: Protest and State Power in the Media Age*. New York: Routledge.

Darlington, R.R. 2006. "The Agitator 'Theory' of Strikes Re-Evaluated." *Labor History* 47(4): 485–509.

Day, Richard. 2005. *Gramsci is Dead: Anarchist Currents in the Newest Social Movements*. Toronto: Between the Lines.

Diehl, Daniel and Mark Donnelly. 2003. *Elbert Hubbard: The Common Sense Revolutionary*. London: Spiro Press.

Dorter, Amanda. 2007. "Mental Health and Mutual Aid in Anarchist Milieus." Paper presented at the "Renewing the Anarchist Tradition" conference, Montpelier, Vermont, November 2–4.

Dyer-Witheford, Nick. 1999. *Cyber Marx: Cycles and Circuits of Struggle in High Technology Capitalism*. Urbana: University of Illinois Press.

Dyer-Witheford, Nick. 2015. *Cyber Proletariat: Global Labour in the Digital Vortex*. London: Pluto.

Early Edition. 2015. "Anonymous: What Is It and How Serious Are Its Threats?" *CBC News*. July 21. http://www.cbc.ca/news/canada/british-columbia/anonymous-what-is-it-and-how-serious-are-its-threats-1.3160906.

Fifth Estate. 2013. "Kicking the Animal out of You." *Fifth Estate* 47(3): 26.

Freedom Center. 2008. Personal communique.

Freeman, Jo and Victoria Johnson (eds.). 1999. *Waves of Protest: Social Movements Since the Sixties*. Lanham, Maryland: Rowman and Littlefield.

Fuchs, Christian and Marisol Sandoval. 2013. *Critique, Social Media and the Information Society*. London: Routledge.

Fuchs, Christian. 2013. *Social Media: A Critical Introduction*. Thousand Oaks: Sage.

Gurr, Ted. 1970. *Why Men Rebel*. Princeton: Princeton University Press.

Harrop, C., P. Trower, and I. Mitchell. 1996. "Does the Biology Go Around the Symptoms?: A Copernican Shift in Schizophrenia Paradigms." *Clinical Psychology Review* 16: 641–654.

Horvath, A. 2002. "President's Letter, Addiction: Disease or Behavior?" http://www.smartrecovery.org/library/Newsletters/PresidentLetters/jul02.pdf.

Icarus Project. 2008. Personal communique.

Jarrett, Kylie. 2015. *Feminism, Labour and Digital Media: The Digital Housewife*. London: Routledge.

Jin, Dal Yong. 2013. *Digital Platforms, Imperialism, and Political Culture*. London: Routledge.

Johnson, Chalmers. 1964. *Revolution and the Social System*. Hoover Institution Studies 3. Palo Alto: The Hoover Institution on War, Revolution, and Peace.

Johnston, Hank. 2011. *States and Social Movements*. London: Polity.

Johnson, Kevin Rashid. 2010. *Defying the Tomb: Selected Prison Writings and Art of Kevin "Rashid" Johnson*. Montreal: Kersplebedeb.

Kinch, Megan. 2013. "Toronto's Free School: It Takes a Community." *Fifth Estate* 47(3): 41–42.

Lomas, Charles. 1968. *The Agitator in American Society*. Englewood Cliffs, NJ: Prentice-Hall.

Ludlow, Peter. 2001. *Crypto Anarchy, Cyberstates, and Pirate Utopia*. Cambridge, MA: MIT Press.

McCally, Micheal. 2002. "Medical Activism and Environmental Health." *Annals of the American Academy of Political and Social Science* 584: 145–158.

Mead, S. and C. MacNeil. 2004. "Peer Support: What Makes it Unique?" www.mentalhealthpeers.com/pdfs/PeerSupportUnique.pdf.

Melucci, A. 1985. "The Symbolic Challenge of Contemporary Movements." *Social Research* 52(4): 789–816.

Nathanson, Constance A. 1999. "Social Movements as Catalysts for Policy Change: The Case of Smoking and Guns." *Journal of Health Politics, Policy and Law* 24(3): 421–488.

Novak, Derry. 2010. "The Place of Anarchism in the History of Political Thought." In *Anarchism as Political Philosophy*, Robert Hoffman (ed.). New Brunswick, NJ: Transaction, 20–33.

Oberschall, Anthony. 1973. *Social Conflict and Social Movements*. Englewood Cliffs, New Jersey: Prentice-Hall.

Rosen, S. 1994. "Beyond Doctors: Workers in Health-Care Reform." *Social Policy*: 40–45.

Sauter, Molly. 2014. *The Coming Swarm: DDOS Actions, Hacktivism, and Civil Disobedience on the Internet*. New York: Bloomsbury.

Scott, James C. 2010. *The Art of Not Being Governed: An Anarchist History of Upland Southeast Asia*. New Haven: Yale University Press.

Shakespeare, T. 1993. "Disabled People's Self-Organization: A New Social Movement?" *Disability Handicap and Society* 8(3): 249–264.

Shantz, Jeff and Jordon Tomblin. 2014. *Cyber Disobedience: Re://Presenting Online Anarchy*. London: Zero Books.

Shantz, Jeff. 2010. *Constructive Anarchy: Building Infrastructures of Resistance*. Farnham: Ashgate.

Walter, J. and J. Peller. 2000. *Recreating Brief Therapy: Preferences and Possibilities*. New York: Norton.

# Index